Techniques for Business Process Redesign

Tying it all Together

Techniques for Business Process Redesign

Tying it all Together

Lynn C. Kubeck

A Wiley–QED Publication

John Wiley & Sons, Inc.

New York • Chichester • Brisbane • Toronto • Singapore

Publisher: K. Schowalter
Editor: B. Elliot
Managing Editor: M. Frederick

Designations used by companies to distinguish their products are often claimed as trademarks. In all instances where John Wiley & Sons, Inc. is aware of a claim, the product names appear in initial capital or all capital letters. Readers, however, should contact the appropriate companies for more complete information regarding trademarks and registration.

This text is printed on acid-free paper.

This publication is designed to provide accurate and authoritative information in regard to the subject matter covered. It is sold with the understanding that the publisher is not engaged in rendering legal, accounting, or other professional service. If legal advice or other expert assistance is required, the services of a competent professional person should be sought.

Library of Congress Cataloging-in-Publication Data:

Kubeck, Lynn C., 1957–
    Techniques for business process redesign : tying it all together/
Lynn C. Kubeck.
      p.   cm.
    "A Wiley/QED Publication."
    Includes index.
    ISBN 0-471-05295-7 (pbk.)
    1. Industrial management.   2. Industrial project management.
3. Organizational change—Management.   I. Title.
HD31.K725   1995
658.4'06—dc20   94-40076
                                             CIP

Printed in the United States of America

10 9 8 7 6 5 4 3 2 1

To Milan for his encouragement and confidence

Contents

Preface

Over the last decade, continuous challenges have been made to traditional business thinking. In the past, the standard mode of operation was larger is better. However, the larger the organization, the slower it is to change. And change has been the buzz word for the 1990s. Many reengineering concepts have been discussed in books and the media for the last few years including software reengineering, business process redesign, business reengineering, information engineering, and work-flow analysis. How does one sort through all of these concepts? How can reengineering concepts be used to help redesign processes within an organization? The goal of this book is twofold:

♦ To help you understand what business process reengineering (BPR) is and why everyone is interested in it
♦ To provide guidance in implementing a BPR project

Now that you know what BPR is and why you would want to pursue it, how to do it is explored in this book.

Chapters 1 and 2 provide background information on what BPR is and why it is an important concept that many organizations are investigating. Chapter 1 provides an overview of the benefits of BPR. It also provides you with an understanding of why process, rather than outcome, is an important concept. Chapter 2 provides an overview of what BPR is and what it isn't. The differences between various types of reengineering projects are discussed, such as software reengineering and information engineering. The differences between BPR projects are also explained. In order to plan and implement a BPR project, it is important to know the type of BPR project being undertaken, thereby understanding the constraints and outcomes that you can expect. Both Chapter 1 and Chapter 2 provide you with background information, concepts, and terminology used throughout the text.

Chapter 3 provides some useful insights on selecting BPR projects, especially first-time projects, and the issues that need to be addressed when contemplating a BPR project. Chapter 4 provides the necessary questions to ask in order to define the BPR project succinctly enough to ensure success.

Chapters 5 through 8 provide a methodology that you can customize to initiate a reengineering project. Using a football analogy, think of Chapters 5 through 8 as the strategies of the game—where the actual plays are determined. These chapters provide readers with a starting point and a methodology from which to customize their own reengineering projects. Pitfalls and suggestions are included throughout the chapters. The goal of this section of the book is to provide an outline of a methodology developed by this author for reengineering projects which can be modified to specific organizational needs. The book provides a higher level of detail or greater abstraction in order to allow the readers to customize the guidelines to their unique situations.

Chapter 9 provides a summary and caveat; it provides some closing thoughts on reengineering projects and addresses the issue of what comes next. After a reengineering project has been undertaken, continuous improvement and evaluation of the reengineering effort are required; these are discussed in detail within this chapter.

Appendix A focuses on techniques that you can use to redesign business processes. These techniques would be analogous to the builder's blueprints. Data flow diagrams and entity-relationship diagrams discussed in Appendix A are the types of available techniques that can be used to redesign and build new automated or manual systems. How these techniques are useful in redesigning business projects and communicating those changes to others within the organization is discussed. Continuing the football analogy, think of Appendix A as the explanation of how to create notations of the plays (methodologies presented in Chapters 5 through 8) in the playbook. An overview of different modeling techniques is also provided. Appendix A illustrates various types of notation and diagramming which can be used to communicate proposed changes in existing processes. Depending on your involvement in the BPR process, you may want to read Appendix A prior to Chapters 5 through 8, since this appendix discusses in more detail techniques introduced in those chapters that help you customize your methodology.

Appendix B focuses on technologies which would be identified as alternative solutions during the transition phase of the BPR project and could possibly be utilized after the redesign process is complete and implementation begins. Appendix B provides the reader with an overview of various available technologies which enable companies to rethink the way they do business. Using the analogy of a builder, the technologies in Appendix B would be analogous to the advent of double-paned insulated windows in the building industry. In the past, when storm windows were necessary, two-story windows were uncommon because of energy loss which was uneconomical. Also, circular or angular windows were not heavily used. Today, many new home designs incorporate two-story windows and arched or angular windows. Without double-paned insulated windows, home designs would not be able to incorporate walls of windows because of heat loss. Just as the double-paned insulated windows allowed the architects to design homes differently, groupware and client/server technology allow business process redesigners to create business systems differently. Imaging capability allows workers miles apart to share and process documents as if they were sitting next to each other. Recalling the football analogy, Appendix B can be compared to the equipment available to the team. This chapter describes these enabling technologies and explains how they can be used as the building blocks to implement redesigned processes.

The express intent of this book is to provide a conceptual understanding of business reengineering as well as provide an outline which can be customized in order to conduct a reengineering project. The scope of any reengineering project is directly correlated to the complexity and level of payback achievable.

This book helps you identify, plan, implement, and assess a BPR project by answering the following questions:

Chapter 1 Introduction and Concepts	Why should I even bother investigating BPR? Is it another fad? What are the benefits of redesigning business processes?
Chapter 2 Introduction and Concepts	What is BPR? What is the difference between BPR and information engineering or software reengineering? Are there different types of BPR projects? How can you identify them? How do they differ? What type of outcomes can be expected from the different types of BPR projects?
Chapter 3 Introduction and Concepts	How do you begin? How do you select a BPR project? Who needs to be involved? Are there any special considerations for a first-time BPR project?
Chapter 4 Introduction and Concepts	After a project has been identified, how do you know if it is a candidate for a BPR project? How do you succinctly define the BPR project in order to ensure success? What is the scope of the project? Has the real problem or issue been identified or merely a symptom of the real problem? How do you tell the difference?
Chapter 5 Business Reengineering Guidelines	How do you plan a BPR project? Who should be involved? What issues need to be addressed? What questions should be asked at the beginning of the project?

Chapter 6 Business Reengineering Guidelines	How do you redesign processes? After a project is identified, defined, and planned, what's next? What are some of the pitfalls that will occur when redesigning processes? Who should be involved in this phase of the project? How do you keep the project on track?
Chapter 7 Business Reengineering Guidelines	After you have redesigned the project conceptually—in other words you know what you want to do—how do you proceed? How do you translate an idea or abstract design into an implementation plan? How will the redesigned process work? What technologies should be applied? How do you decide which technological alternatives to use in the redesigned process? Who is involved in this transitional phase of the BPR project? If team members change, how is continuity maintained?
Chapter 8 Business Reengineering Guidelines	How do you implement the redesigned process? What issues need to be addressed before changes are made? What types of issues and concerns will be raised by staff as well as management? Who should be involved?
Chapter 9 Recap	How do you ensure that the redesigned process will not become stagnant, needing to be redesigned again? How do you introduce change within an organization? What types of issues need to be addressed relative to changing the way things are done? What are some caveats that you need to be aware of?
Appendix A Techniques and Tools	What techniques are available to help redesign business processes? How do you keep track of all of the details in a BPR project? How do you ensure that everyone understands the process and how it will be redesigned, since in most instances you are dealing with abstract issues (policies, procedures, and information flows)?
Appendix B Techniques and Tools	What technologies are available to enable business processes to be redesigned? How are some of these technologies being used?

ACKNOWLEDGMENTS

I would like to thank Candace Maicher for her willingness to read and critique the manuscript. As a reader, you will directly benefit from her efforts to make this book more readable.

I also want to thank my family, especially Milan, David, and Samantha, for their continued support during the writing of this book which has been a formidable challenge.

PART I

Introduction and Concepts

Automate, Integrate, or Obliterate?

Today's computers are faster, less expensive, and have greater storage capacity, so why don't we just automate all of our existing processes? In fact, that's what has been happening since the advent of the computer! Manual processes, many of which were not efficient to begin with, were automated. The idea of placing new technology in an outmoded infrastructure is not new; it is traditionally the way new technologies have evolved.

TECHNOLOGY AS AN ENABLER

For instance, when electricity was first introduced into the manufacturing environment to replace steam engines, there was no immediate change in the manufacturing processes or the underlying infrastructure of manufacturing plants. One technology was simply substituted for another, with no major changes to the infrastructure taking place. Prior to the invention of electric motors, buildings were designed with multiple floors in order to conserve the steam energy; this was efficient energy conservation. However, it was very inefficient from a materials handling and personnel standpoint. The product had to be moved up and down between floors to complete the manufacturing process which was labor-intensive. However, the infrastructure made sense. Multiple machines could be powered by a single steam engine; it was not feasible to install a steam engine in each machine. When electric motors were initially introduced, they were incorporated into the existing infrastructure. An electric motor simply replaced the steam engine with no other changes made. Multiple machines were still powered by a single engine; however, instead of steam power, electric power was the source of energy.

Productivity improvements did not occur in this process until approximately 40 years after electric motors started replacing steam-powered motors. This was because initially, when electric motors replaced steam motors, the machines and buildings were still designed in the same manner— using a single power source for multiple machines. Once the breakthrough idea occurred that separate, smaller engines could be placed in each machine, the constraint of locating all machines within close proximity to each other was eliminated. Low-cost motorized engines were placed in each machine—allowing machines to be located anywhere in the factory. This eliminated the architectural constraint that buildings needed to have multiple floors in order to conserve the steam power. Buildings were then designed to provide efficient use of personnel and materials handling rather than optimizing machine location in order to conserve steam energy. Buildings no longer needed to be designed around the steam engine. Infrastructures could be designed around the processes optimizing personnel usage. The buildings were designed long and flat, on one level, in order to minimize moving the product up and down between floors. New techniques for inventory control and materials handling were introduced which would not have been possible in a narrow multifloored building. Productivity started increasing.

However, the introduction of the technology, in this case the electric motor, did not *cause* the changes to take place— it *allowed* the changes to occur. If history repeats itself, we should be on the verge of productivity improvements for office work *caused* by the invention of the computer. Technology *allows* change or process redesign to take place, but does not necessarily *cause* it to occur.

PRODUCTIVITY PARADOX IN THE OFFICE

The computer was introduced to the business world in the 1960s, even though it was invented earlier. Over the past 40 years computers have been replacing processes previously done manually or by mechanical adding machines and typewriters. The functions or processes themselves have not changed; the technology has just been applied to the way things have always been done, similar to replacing the steam-driven motor with an electric one without changing the infrastructure. For instance, today secretaries use computers rather than typewriters to type letters. However, in many instances, the manager still dictates the letter to some type of dictation device and the secretary still *types* the letter into the computer, printing off a draft for the manager's review. Replacing the typewriter with a computer in this scenario did not add any type of productivity improvement. One technology (typewriter) was simply replaced by another technology (the computer) and inserted into an existing process. The process itself, in this case business communications, must be reevaluated as well as the technologies that are related to it for productivity improvement to take place. In other words, the process of generating business letters, or more generally, business communications in all forms should be evaluated—not just the technology of printing the letters via typewriter or computer.

Of course, computers are and continue to be used for innovation and a myriad of business applications. However, almost any office you walk into today will be arranged in the same way it was before the introduction of the computer and much of the work will be done the same. The office has not been drastically altered by the introduction of desktop computers. Of course, high-tech computers have replaced typewriters, and fax machines, copiers, and other technologies abound. However, in many cases the secretary is still sitting in front of the boss's office, the clerical support staff is still centrally located together, and everyone still works from 9:00 A.M. to 5:00 P.M. With new technologies such as telecommunications and portable computers the traditional office setup is no longer a necessity, just as electric motorized machines did not have to be located physically close to each other. Computers and other technologies can allow office changes to occur; however, the mere existence of these technologies does not mean that any changes necessarily will occur.

Process versus Product

Dropping new technologies into an old infrastructure will not necessarily provide productivity breakthroughs. Replacing steam engines with electric motors without redesigning the infrastructure or replacing typewriters with computers without redesigning the office communications process will not provide major productivity improvements. Some gains in productivity will be realized; however, the technology by itself cannot provide the types of productivity gains necessary in today's global marketplace. The processes themselves must be evaluated rather than focusing on the technologies used to implement them.

Articles in almost any publication espouse the view that productivity in the information-based sector has not increased in past years. Computers have been placed on almost every desktop in large corporations and mainframe systems have churned out incredible volumes of written statistics and documentation. But the bottom line is that productivity has not gone up for office-based work, while productivity in manufacturing has been on the rise. The answer to this dilemma lies in where the focus has been placed. Manufacturing redesign projects have historically focused on the process of manufacturing itself, using technology to enable them to make the necessary changes to the process. However, the focus never wavered from the process itself. Business process redesign applied to office work, on the other hand, has started out studying the process, in some instances; however, the focus of many of these projects tended to shift toward technology implementation.

Office work, in the context of this book, constitutes all non-manufacturing endeavors from executive decision-making to accounting and sales to word processing and electronic mail. Vendors that can sell you the software and/or hardware to solve just about any office business problem are abundant. However, the focus of a project often drifts toward implementing technology rather than analyzing and improving the process, which limits the productivity gains of the project.

For example, if sales are down in an organization, a typical first solution is to install a customer-tracking software package which will keep track of contacts and generate follow-up letters. In this scenario, a solution has been provided without fully understanding and defining the problem. This is a typical course of action when solving business issues. The technology is offered as a panacea, rather than focusing on the underlying process, in this case, obtaining new clients and increasing sales. The problem may very well be that the sales staff needs training, because they do not fully understand all of the benefits of the product or service they are selling; therefore, they cannot successfully market it to their customers. There may be a myriad of personnel or procedural, process-driven, problems which have caused sales to decrease. The danger in looking to technology to solve those problems is that the problems still exist after technology is applied to the situation; they are merely covered up by a layer or layers of technology. The organization, with the automated contact management software, can keep track of statistics and generate letters to prospective clients. But they still do not know whether the information they are providing their clients is sufficient or why sales have gone down. If you are very lucky you will hit upon the right technology solution to your problem, if your focus is not on the process but on applying technologies, and ultimately solve your problem. In most cases, however, the problem will persist until it is directly addressed.

Manufacturing versus Office

Factories have implemented computer integrated manufacturing (CIM) to assist with the production process. Robotics have been introduced on the production line with statistical sampling being done automatically throughout the production process, alerting management to any variations in product quality. One major point is that as technology was being applied to the production process, the actual production process itself was being reevaluated and redefined. *Technology was not applied to the existing processes—the processes were redesigned to take advantage of the technology.* This is an extremely important point, not just semantics. Production and quality were increased while costs were decreased by focusing on the *process* rather than the *product*.

Returning to the previously mentioned organization with low sales, the company's focus needs to shift from product to process. In this case, the product is the number of sales made. This can be measured statistically; the software solution they have adopted can help them track this information. However, will this solve the problem of reduced sales? It won't if they don't shift their attention from product (number of sales) to process (how sales are made). Studying different methods of how new clients have been generated over the years, not only within their organization, but also within like institutions around the country, or even the globe, will prove more beneficial. Contact management software is a great tool, if used properly. However, any technology by itself, without changing the underlying procedures and business processes within the office, will not solve the business problems under investigation. The focus must remain on the process, without straying to look at new technologies as a panacea to solve the problems.

This trend of focusing on the process rather than the product or outcome has not been realized in the office environment. One major difference between manufacturing and office work is the level of repetitiveness. Manufacturing is an iterative process with clear rules defining what is an acceptable product and what is not. The process is often much easier to identify and to stay focused on. If you are making steel, there are certain steps that must follow in sequential order for the product to be produced correctly. The process itself is physical: You can see the actual transformation from the initial steps of the process to the end result. Because of this tangible aspect of steel production, or any manufacturing process for that matter, it is easier to conceptualize and focus on the process. The processes involved in office work are not as easily identifiable and definable.

Office Work

Office work does not consist of one type of work. There are several functions that the term office work encompasses such as marketing, accounting, finance, sales, and information processing to name a few. Within every functional area of office work certain processes take place:

♦   Document preparation/word processing
♦   Business communications
♦   Problem solving
♦   Decision-making
♦   Order processing
♦   Strategic planning

The term office work is a misnomer since it spans the range of clerical or support functions to executive or decision-making functions. Office work can be defined by two dimensions—ability to reproduce functions or tasks and the level of frequency of occurrence (i.e., daily, weekly, or annually). Figure 1.1 illustrates examples of tasks which can be classified using the two dimensions of frequency of occurrence and level of repetitiveness. Note that trying to group all of these functions under the heading of office work is one of the reasons there is such discrepancy about what type of automation tools are needed for office work and why productivity has not been increasing. Also, without a clear definition of what type of office work is involved for a specific problem, it is difficult to focus on the process rather than the product (outcome). If we can't define the term

Types of Office Functions

Frequency/ Level of Repetitiveness	Daily	Weekly/ Monthly	Annually
Highly Repetitive	Order Processing	Payroll, Billing	Tax Returns, Inventory
Partially Reproducable	Sales Letters, Mailings	Trend Forecasting, What if Analysis	Annual Reports
Unique	Problem Solving	Ad Hoc Reporting	Strategic Planning

Figure 1.1   Functions of office work.

office work more succinctly, how can we expect to increase efficiency and productivity?

Productivity of Workers

"White-collar" worker productivity has held constant over the last few decades. "Blue-collar" productivity has increased since the introduction of computers in manufacturing and computers have been introduced into both the office and the manufacturing areas of organizations. However, many manufacturing tasks previously done manually have been automated—saving money, increasing quality and accuracy. The same productivity gains have not been realized in the office. Though office work is not the same as factory work, the same concepts for automation have been applied; but manufacturing has increased productivity because, over the years, *processes* have changed.

The technology initially introduced, such as the steam engine example cited earlier, has taken hold and innovative ways to change the manufacturing process have been realized. Technology is not the major productivity breakthrough in and of itself, but enables processes to change in order to increase productivity. The introduction of the computer in the office, particularly at the secretary's desk did not provide for any major productivity gains because the processes and procedures remained the same in the office. Unless underlying processes change, replacing a typewriter with a computer will not prove to be an effective method of applying technology to an organization in order to increase productivity or quality.

However, if you look at the processes and functions performed in an office and redesign those functions using technology as an enabling tool, major breakthroughs could take place. The key concepts here are that technology should serve in the role of enabler, rather than the focal point of any business process redesign (BPR) project. Technologies exist today that could enable major changes and ultimately bring major cost savings, if implemented correctly. Correct implementation means—change the process and use the technology to that extent. (Appendix A identifies some of the current technologies which are changing the way we do business.) However, the focus on the process, rather than on the technology must be maintained. New technologies are very enticing and the allure of using them to solve business problems is great. However, the real benefits are obtained, not by applying glamorous new technologies to existing processes, but by changing underlying processes and possibly applying new technologies to these redesigned processes. With the advent of telecommunications, mobile computing, and the Information Highway, does an office need to be defined by a physical location or building? What type of cost savings as well as quality issues can be derived once physical location is no longer a constraint when assessing how you do business?

To Automate or Not to Automate—That is the Question

We need to break out of the mind set that automation is always the solution. Without changing underlying processes (the way things are done), substituting new technologies for existing ones will not provide any benefit.

♦   If you replace a horse-drawn wagon with a truck, yet do not change the process of how the farmer uses the truck, he will simply hook the horse to the truck in order to pull it and no productivity improvement will occur.

♦   Using the same logic, if you replace the secretary's typewriter with a computer, yet do not provide the training to change the way in which the machine is used, no benefit will occur. The secretary will continue to type the written document in the same way. The capabilities of the technology will not be used and ultimately no productivity gains will occur.

Technology provides the tools which enable change to processes and procedures to occur; but, it is not an end in itself. Without changing the underlying business processes, applying new technology to existing processes will not improve productivity, and in many instances may actually hinder it. When Mike Hammer's *Harvard Review* article was published in 1990, the business world began to murmur about reengineering business processes. Five years later, almost every businessperson has heard the term, even though it has many definitions and many other concepts, such as work-flow analysis and continuous quality improvement, have become entwined with it. Why is this concept so appealing to business?

♦   Traditionally the decision between cutting costs or increasing service was required

♦   Service could not be increased without adding costs such as additional people or more technological equipment

♦   Costs could not be reduced without cutting services or sacrificing quality

However, business process redesign offers business the opportunity to cut costs and, at the same time, increase service. Certainly, this is a noble goal to strive for.

Molding Future Management

It is a paradox why more organizations haven't embraced business process redesign. One reason is the way in which future managers are trained—not only formally within colleges and universities, but also on the job—and learning by example as well.

☑ *Formal Training*

Beginning with college courses and continuing through management training programs, would-be managers are taught to *control* current processes. In universities, courses explaining theories about motivating workers, methods for controlling budgets, and techniques for controlling processes are taught. Most college management curriculums include some form of statistical analysis for quality control purposes which teaches how to incrementally improve a given process. This is an important skill, given that the underlying process is sound to begin with. Quality control courses do not, however, in any way suggest making radical changes to a given process. Most quality control courses are focused on manufacturing processes and do not even address business procedures and processes.

Information systems analysis and design courses also stress that major changes should not be undertaken. When "redesigning" a computer information system the user's needs should be obtained. However, the analyst should not question the rationale behind the user's requested needs. College information systems analysis courses teach that if the user requires duplicate information, or any other requirement, the job of the analyst is to gather those requirements, not question their merit. Because of this type of formal training, managers are being

taught not to question existing processes. Systems analysts are also being taught not to question management's
or the end user's requirements or needs.

☑ *On-the-job Training*

After graduating from college the next logical progression in would-be managers' careers is a management
training program with a large organization. Here they
learn *the way things are done* within the company. They
learn what processes are in place and how to maneuver
politically within the company. Future managers are
taught "not to rock the boat." Nowhere in this process
are would-be managers taught to critically assess the
processes and procedures already in place and investigate alternatives.

☑ *Learning by Example*

In most large organizations risk-taking is not encouraged. If a manager dramatically changes the way things
are done successfully, that manager is generally rewarded. However, what happens if the change is not successful? In most organizations, the manager would be
demoted or relieved of that position altogether. If major
changes and improvements are to take place, failure
must be tolerated. The old adage that a manager who
never makes a mistake hasn't done anything is true in
relationship to redesign efforts. For the new manager,
"rocking the boat" depends on how an organization deals
with failed procedural changes and risk-taking.

If the would-be managers take an entrepreneurial career
path, they may develop innovative procedures initially, unless they model their business from an established business
in the same line of work. Entrepreneurs are more apt to radically change an established process or procedure. They do not
have the luxury of substantial assets backing their endeavors; however, they also do not have a great deal of overhead
and history with which to deal. Because of their limited re-

sources these entrepreneurs must be innovative and creative in order to stay competitive. In a small organization, risk-taking is encouraged making it a fertile environment for business process redesign and continuous improvement.

Change versus Control

Controlling current processes while trying to squeeze extra productivity out of them is becoming futile. It is similar to trying to squeeze a few more miles out of an old economy car. At some point, you need to disregard the existing base (old car or current process) and start new (new car or redesigned process). In order for major productivity improvements to occur, major changes to existing processes must occur. Using the previous analogy, the car must be replaced. Even with the most motivated work force and the newest technologies, if the underlying business process being undertaken is not reassessed periodically, efficiency and effectiveness will eventually stop increasing and changes will become more expensive. This effect can be illustrated by examining the deregulation of the transportation industry in the 1980s.

The transportation industry, specifically, truck lines, enjoyed handsome profits servicing markets that were protected by the lack of competition before deregulation. Prior to 1980, it was difficult and expensive to obtain "authority" from the government to become a trucking company. When deregulation was enacted in the early 1980s, authority became easy to obtain. Soon there were many new, smaller, and more competitive truck lines around. They were creating niche markets for themselves by specializing in specific areas formerly serviced by the old, established transportation companies. The new truck lines were not only moving the product at reduced rates, but were also giving the customer better service. With this new competition and a slumping economy, the majority of the old, established truck lines disappeared.

Throughout the deregulation process, the established truck lines tried to "tweak" their existing processes. They tried to motivate workers to do a little more each day—squeezing additional productivity out of existing processes.

As history proves, this approach will not work in the long run. Eventually, productivity cannot continue to increase if processes remain the same. At some point, new ideas and new ways of doing business will prevail. The success of the new truck lines was their ability to focus their processes on the primary customer—the purchaser of their services (see Figure 1.2). They were able to customize their service, something the established truck lines had not attempted.

Not every industry has encountered these extraordinary circumstances, but a great many changes have occurred since the early 1980s. The advent of the personal computer is one.

♦   In what ways have these changes affected how companies do business?
♦   Did the steps taken by companies to address these changes
   ◊   increase productivity,
   ◊   service the customer better,
   ◊   or provide a Band-Aid approach solution?

These are the types of questions which drive companies to investigate business process redesign.

PRESSURES ON TODAY'S ORGANIZATIONS

The current environment in which business exists is global and highly competitive. Organizations no longer have the luxury of continuing to be profitable while inefficiencies exist. The computer has been an integral part of organizations since the 1970s, with the advent of the personal computer and computer networks in the 1980s, even more corporate personnel have access to computers. With all this investment in computer hardware and software, why hasn't office-centered productivity increased? Two reasons are:

♦   The focus needs to be on the process, not the outcome
♦   Technology is an enabler, not a panacea

Aside from heavy competition, organizations today are faced with consumers demanding higher quality products

The primary customer varies for each organization. Any organization can have a multitude of customer types. However, there can only be one primary customer if the organization wants to customize their services. That primary customer should be focused on when any decisions related to changing business processes are made. For example, if a hotel serves both convention clientele as well as vacationers, the focus of their service will be different depending on which is identified as their primary customer. The concept of primary customer can also apply to internal departments.

For example, an information technology department within a university can have several customers (faculty, students, and administrative staff). How the primary customer has been identified affects the type of procedures and services the department provides. Whenever changes to existing processes or services are contemplated, it is important to identify the primary customer, and ensure that all individuals involved are in agreement as to who the primary customer is.

Figure 1.2   Primary customer.

and better customer service. Companies differentiate themselves from their competition through:

♦ Customer service initiatives
♦ Ability to customize their services and products
♦ Higher quality products

How does a company increase service and quality and stay competitive? Many companies look toward BPR principals and techniques to help answer this question. Only you can determine if BPR is worth investigating and implementing.

♦ Is it worth the time to investigate a concept that can help increase service and quality while reducing costs in order to be competitive?

BUILDING ON OLD SYSTEMS

Over the years, procedures and processes have been developed within an organization to provide a means to cope with both internal and external changes to the organization. In effect current procedures have been built upon existing procedures and constraints and so on. Procedures that were developed in the past to accommodate a certain legal requirement or idiosyncrasy of an existing system may not be necessary any more. New procedures have been built upon the old and many times the question, "Why are we even doing this in the first place?" is never asked. Computer specialists are quick to point out that they could automate or enhance the existing process and reduce time and money. You cannot be more productive while simultaneously cutting costs if you continually build upon the unstable foundation of old systems. The following questions need to be asked:

♦ Should we provide this service or perform this process?
♦ Do we need this procedure?
♦ Could we provide this service in a different/better manner?

Many companies were told that if they bought into the idea of the computer revolution and the information age, they would automatically receive efficiency gains. This hasn't happened because, as any programmer knows, the axiom "garbage in—garbage out" is true for systems development. If existing systems (manual procedures and processes) are automated without looking deeper to see how technology could enable breakthrough applications and techniques, an automated system which mirrors the manual system will be the outcome. The ramifications of mirroring manual systems or previously existing automated systems is that the constraints and limitations of the existing systems are built into the new system—even if the constraints or limitations are no longer valid today.

The unstable foundation old systems may be built upon could be either manual or automated processes which have been accomplished without change over the years. Anyone who has ever dealt with government agencies, especially recorder's offices, can relate to the mounds of paperwork and manual processes that have been in place for many years without change. Many times organizations automate or update computer programs that are based on obsolete procedures and processes. The assumption is that the underlying processes upon which the computer programs were written must still be sound. This assumption is not valid. The technology of computers themselves has changed, the business environment has changed, and government regulations have changed. Can any organization afford to continue with the assumption that what was done in the past is appropriate for today?

The Impact of Automating Current Systems

The major concern of automating or updating current systems is payback. Whether it will be worth the effort is paramount in the minds of management. Too many things have changed since legacy systems were written. Legacy systems are those computer systems which usually run on a mainframe computer developed 10, 20, or 30 years ago. Today, most of the automation issues revolve around updating these systems rather than automating manual processes. Legacy systems are expensive to maintain and modification to them is a programmer's nightmare, as well as an inordinate expense to the organization. Many companies have opted to leave well enough alone and continue to use the systems; however, with sky-rocketing maintenance costs—both software and hardware—the issue to update these systems will not go away. However, where does one begin when analyzing legacy systems? Concentrate on the *what* not the *how* of the system. You need to look beyond how the current system is designed to what the essence of the system is. The consequences of using the existing legacy system as the starting point for designing a new system is that constraints, limitations, and problems inherent in the legacy system will be designed into the new system.

Remember, you don't want to build your new processes on top of existing processes that may no longer be necessary. For example, if an existing process requires two copies of a purchase requisition to be created—one forwarded to the purchasing department and the other maintained by central administration—do not automate this process without questioning why two copies are necessary. Do not assume that whatever currently is in place must remain in place. After further investigation, it may be determined that two copies were necessary in the past because the offices (purchasing and central administration) were physically separated and both needed to obtain the information on the requisition upon request. With today's technology, the physical constraints of the legacy system may not be an issue. If the new process was developed assuming that duplicate information needed to be sent to both departments, the medium in which the information is received may change, but both departments would still need to deal with the information. If the constraint that caused two separate documents to be created no longer exists, what is the benefit of continuing the procedure? Look not only to automate processes, but to obliterate them as well. Reduce the number of tasks and processes required whenever feasible. In many instances if you do not find out why a process or procedure is done in a certain manner, you are only getting rid of a symptom of the problem—similar to relieving a symptom of an illness—the disease still exists.

Solving Symptoms Rather than Problems

The hardest part of any problem-solving scenario is defining the problem exactly. Most times symptoms quickly become evident—however, it is imperative to dig deeper to find the root of the problem. This scenario is analogous to pulling a weed out of your garden. If you find creative ways to pull the weed but still leave the root in the ground, the weed will come back. Similarly, if you solve various symptoms of the problem without solving the actual problem itself, the symptoms will keep recurring, maybe in slightly different variations, because the problem hasn't been solved. You need to get to the root of the problem.

The side effects of solving symptoms rather than problems are numerous. Many unnecessary information systems developed in the past were solutions to symptoms; once the problem is resolved, the computer system solving the symptom is no longer necessary. With the cost of computer systems development, and the increased complexity of integrated information systems and technologies, organizations cannot afford to develop computer information systems that are not necessary (solving symptoms rather than problems). Spending time to determine the actual nature of the problem is time well spent. Otherwise time and money are devoted to developing systems, manual or automated, that address a symptom that will not alleviate the problem. The question that needs to be asked is "Why are we even investigating improving, redesigning, or changing this system or process?" Constantly question why an issue is a problem. By taking an investigative, questioning approach, you have a better opportunity to uncover the underlying problem and address it head on.

How much time and money could be saved by eliminating unnecessary procedures and processes rather then spending time trying to make them more efficient? Efficiency without effectiveness is futile. A thorough investigation of what the problem is and the causes and effects associated with it is necessary rather than putting a band-aid on the problem. This is where business process redesign concepts can be applied to determine where valuable resources should be expended. Chapter 4 addresses this vital concept in greater detail.

Speeding Up Ineffectiveness

Automating unnecessary processes prevents uncovering the actual underlying problems in many cases. If ineffective processes are automated, they can be done quicker and with less resources. Therefore the ineffective processes are never questioned. In effect, however, automation has merely provided a buffer or hidden problems from management's view. It is only after ineffective system is layered upon ineffective system that the issue is even raised again—"What problem were we trying to solve?" The computer revolution has not given us the paperless office which was supposed to happen in the 1980s—instead we have more paper, reports, and useless information spewing from our computers than ever before.

Whenever a system seems to generate a considerable amount of data, the tendency is to assume it is a necessary and vital part of the organization. This is not always the case. The ability to generate useless paper can be accelerated which can be a problem in itself. The computer has allowed us to create more and more paper at faster speeds. Without taking the time to determine if we really need this data, we may be perpetuating the inefficiencies. As stated earlier, the much heralded "paperless" office has not become a reality. One reason is that computers have only replaced manual processes, enabling faster turnaround time. They have not, however, changed the way we do business. More paper does not mean more efficiency.

Business needs have changed faster than the central IS (Information Systems) department could address. This has caused a growing IS programming backlog. Most companies have programming requests planned for implementation for at least the next five years. This programming backlog coupled with the accelerated changes in the business environment have forced business units to determine alternative methods of obtaining the information they need. Departmental units have created their own mini information systems, processes, and procedures (see Figure 1.3). Because available technology provides faster turnaround time, many processes currently existing in organizations are fraught with redundant data entry and needless repetition between departments or business units. Rather than perpetuating this trend, the underlying issues must be addressed. Certain information needs to be centralized, while

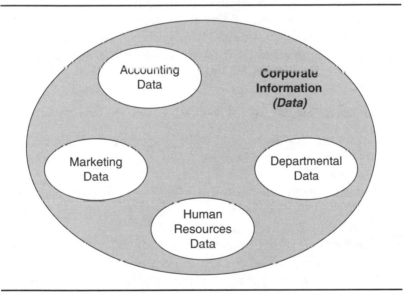

Figure 1.3 Islands of information occur when various departments or subgroups within an organization create their own database. There is some data that can be maintained at a departmental level; however, any data that needs to be shared by more than one department should be centralized in order to ensure that redundant information is not maintained. The problem of islands of information has occurred because of the backlog of programming requests in most information systems departments. It is an issue that needs to be addressed when redesigning processes. Many times the symptom versus problem issue is related to pockets or islands of information existing within an organization.

ion can be localized or departmentalized.
rstanding the overall processes involved and
ie various departments is critical in order to
ere the information should reside.

process redesign and information engineering
concepts provide the ability to use technology in a way which
will enable major changes in business procedures or processes and take into account the needs of the entire organization. Rather than perpetuating islands of information and/
or automation within an organization, the focus needs to be
how the information will be used within the entire organization. Many companies are realizing that their information is
a corporate asset and how they manage their internal processes and procedures can be the determining factor of
whether they succeed in the fast-paced global 1990s and
beyond. Instead of just doing things right, we need to *do the
right things right* and BPR helps to address these issues.

CHAPTER HIGHLIGHTS

- Replacing one technology with another without changing the underlying business processes will not increase
  productivity.
- Technology by itself cannot increase productivity. Technology, as an enabler, can allow processes to change,
  thereby increasing productivity.
- The focus of a BPR project needs to be on the process, not
  the outcome, or the enabling technology.
- Historically, manufacturing productivity improvement
  projects have focused on the process which is why they
  have been successful and productivity in manufacturing
  has improved over the years.
- Conversely, office productivity has not improved over the
  years mainly because the emphasis has been on automating existing processes and applying technologies,
  rather than critically evaluating current business processes and procedures, and changing them.

- ✎ Technology will not solve a business process problem. Technology can allow changes to occur, but is not a panacea.
- ✎ Technology applied to symptoms, rather than problems, can temporarily hide the underlying problems. However, the problem is not solved and will surface at another time, possibly as a different symptom.
- ✎ It is easier to identify processes within a manufacturing environment because of the repetitive nature of the work. It is more difficult to identify processes in office work.
- ✎ Office work is not a single, easily defined commodity. It encompasses many different aspects of work from highly repetitive, frequently done work to decision-making which is nonrepetitive and nonscheduled. Tasks are constantly redefined and needs constantly changing. Processes are more abstract.
- ✎ The term office work is a misnomer since it spans the range of clerical or support functions to executive or decision-making functions.
- ✎ Business process redesign offers business the opportunity to cut costs and, at the same time, increase service.
- ✎ One reason why business process redesign (business reengineering) has not been embraced more readily by organizations is the manner in which future managers are trained (formal training, on-the-job training, and learning by example). Controlling existing processes is stressed and risk-taking is discouraged.
- ✎ The primary customer should be identified before any redesign effort is undertaken. What clientele is identified as the primary customer will determine the products and services offered by the organization.
- ✎ BPR is not a cookbook approach or another term for applying technology to existing processes. BPR is a method whereby organizations take a hard look at the way they are doing business and determine whether current processes should be automated, integrated with other processes, or eliminated.
- ✎ New procedures are built upon old procedures in many

instances and the question "Why are we even doing this in the first place?" is never asked.

✎ Pressures on today's businesses force the issue of investigating BPR. Global competition and a changing business environment are two prominent issues why BPR is appealing to organizations.

What Is Business Reengineering?

In order to discuss business reengineering or business process redesign, it is necessary to understand related terminology. The term reengineering covers many different processes, from redesigning software to redefining the functions of the business. The interchanging of these terms in many publications leads to confusion. Magazine articles celebrate how various organizations have reengineered their businesses. Software vendors boast how their applications will enable you to reengineer your business. In reality, the term "reengineering" can mean different things to different individuals and organizations. An understanding of what reengineering and BPR are, as well as the different types of reengineering projects that exist will help to sort through the semantics.

BUSINESS REENGINEERING—A PERSPECTIVE

Before you can determine whether you want to use BPR methods to redefine processes, you should understand what BPR is.

- One way to define a concept is to explain what it is not.
    - ◊ Business process redesign is not another term for simply automating existing processes or systems.

◇ Business process redesign is not a cookbook approach to business problem-solving.
♦ Business process redesign combines methodologies and techniques from information systems analysis, management, organizational behavior, and communication disciplines.
♦ Business process redesign is a method whereby organizations can take a good hard look at the way they do business and reevaluate their effectiveness.
♦ Business process redesign focuses on the process—not the product or outcome.
♦ Business process redesign as a methodology analyzes business processes in order to determine whether to automate, integrate, or obliterate each process.

TYPES OF REENGINEERING PROJECTS

There are various types of projects which can be confused with business reengineering projects. It is important to understand the type of project which is being considered in order to determine the level of change that may occur, as well as the scope of the project. You can then determine who should be involved in the project and what type of recommendations will be generated.

Software Reengineering

Software reengineering describes redesigning or porting software from one computer platform to another. The purpose of the software is not changed; only the characteristics that allow it to operate on a certain computer platform are altered. This is similar to translating a book from one language to another. The meaning and content are not changed; only the words used to convey the message are altered. In other words, software reengineering does not take into account the underlying business processes currently in place within an organization. Software reengineering only extends to the scope of the software application or applications constituting one computer system. For example, a software re-engineering project may include a payroll system currently in place within an organization. The scope of the project will include the inputs and outputs from the current system; however, it will not take into account the business procedures or policies surrounding the payroll process or even other applications which may obtain information or provide information to the system. A human resources system which provides data to the payroll system would be outside the scope of the project. There are various levels of software engineering projects: restructuring code, reverse engineering, and reengineering design specifications. All types of software reengineering projects will require extensive computer systems personnel involvement.

Restructuring Code

If the project begins by focusing on an application or set of applications, chances are it is some form of a software reengineering project. Currently, many tools are available to assist organizations with structuring their existing legacy code. Legacy systems and their applications code, are a major problem for today's corporations. In many cases, legacy systems were developed before structured programming and structured analysis were available. The program may consist of unstructured code, "spaghetti-code," which is very difficult and costly to maintain. In most cases this unstructured code which is usually mainframe COBOL programming code, can be restructured to provide limited benefit. Restructuring the code will provide some efficiencies in maintenance; however, no new functionality is gained regardless of whether it remains on the mainframe system. With the existing trend toward downsizing, there is a good probability that, in the future, the restructured code will need to be ported to another platform if it is not done so at the time the software reengineering occurs. With the legacy code restructured, it is easier to use translating utilities and other tools to rewrite the code into another language in order to run the programs on a downsized platform.

Reverse Engineering

Reverse engineering is another concept that uses the existing code as a starting point; however, it extends beyond just restructuring the program code. Utility programs are available to assist with this process. Many integrated-computer assisted software engineering (I-CASE) products address this issue, but, at this point in time, there are no tools that can take existing legacy code and translate it into design specifications with 100 percent accuracy. This is the direction that I-CASE vendors are moving toward. Also, once models have been developed in the I-CASE tool, redesign can be accomplished at the conceptual level, prior to programming. In other words, modifications can be made in the I-CASE models and code generated from the I-CASE tool without having to modify the program code.

This allows software reengineering to occur at the design specification level rather than at the program level. Design specifications can be thought of as a recipe with the program code as the entree created from the recipe. It is much easier to make changes to a specific entree at the recipe level than to try to determine what ingredients and in what quantities they exist in the entree and extrapolating this information in order to change the recipe.

Reengineering Design Specifications

Reengineering design specifications addresses the logic behind the actual programs, the recipe behind the entree. It extends beyond restructuring the program code. Reengineering design specifications has a broader scope than just the software. The design of the system contains the information about why the system was developed in the first place, the flows of information between various departments or computer systems. However, in order to undertake this type of project the design specifications for the system under review must be available. Documentation such as data flow diagrams, system flow charts, and system requirements must be available in order to be used as a starting point. This is the type of documentation that I-CASE tools provide.

Although this type of project is similar to reverse engineering projects, the starting point is the design specifications rather than the code. This would be analogous to redesigning a building by either starting with the blueprints (reengineering design specifications) or touring the house and developing the design specifications in order to change them (reverse engineering). Many projects are either reverse engineering or reengineering design specifications rather than true business process redesign projects. It is important to understand the difference because any type of software reengineering project will:

♦ Be limited in the amount of change that can occur within policies and procedures.
♦ Focus on the computer programs rather than policies and procedures, possibly causing a misunderstanding to occur as to the outcome of the project.

Software Engineering versus Software Reengineering

Software *reengineering* is different from software *engineering*. Software engineering is a disciplined approach to engineering software—developing computer systems in a more disciplined approach. In the past, programming was looked upon as a type of art form. A programmer in the 1970s was an artist, creatively solving problems by developing applications programs (software). However, as critical computer systems became prevalent, more emphasis was placed on controlling software development. As more and more critical business applications relied on software, the viewpoint that writing software was an art form began to fade. Software development needed to address many of the issues that various engineering disciplines address such as consistency, reliability, maintainability, and the ability to effectively share information with various team members. Software development needed to become more sophisticated in order to develop and maintain complex, mission-critical applications.

Software engineering addresses the issue of developing software much in the same way that any engineering discipline addresses development issues related to end product.

The thinking has shifted from viewing programming as a creative, artistic endeavor to seeing it as a more scientific, engineering one. Software engineering is a technique that can be used within a software reengineering project or any type of software development project. Software *reengineering*, in essence seeks to understand the logic of existing software and convert it, using software *engineering* standards, to a new language or platform.

Information Engineering

Information engineering is a methodology popularized by James Martin. Information engineering focuses on the automated system, similar to software reengineering; however, the scope extends beyond computer applications. Software reengineering and information engineering differ in their emphasis.

◆   Software reengineering focuses on the existing application code.
◆   Information engineering focuses on the existing data input and output from the system.

Information engineering only evaluates and analyzes the existing software applications when it is necessary to understand how certain output data is derived. Emphasis is placed on *what the current system is doing—not how it is doing it*. This statement is not an exercise in semantics. The major difference between *what* and *how* something is done relates to the level of abstraction on which the project focuses.

To understand *what* a system does, it is not necessary to understand every line of code. In fact, the applications may be viewed as a "black box." The term "black box" actually originated in engineering disciplines, but has been used in software development. The concept of the black box is analogous to a fax machine. You know what information you put into the machine, such as the phone number and information to be sent. You also know what information comes out of the fax machine, such as the information sent along with a transaction log or receipt to let you know the information was sent. Applications programs can be viewed in the same way as a fax machine or telephone. You know what information or data needs to be put into the application and what information will come out; however, you do not have to know how it works. Just as you can use a fax machine without understanding data communications theory and how the actual fax machine converts the written data into electronic signals and sends it across telephone wires, you can use an application without understanding the programming logic behind that application.

Similarly, most people do not understand, nor need to understand, how the telephone actually works in order to discuss how it could be used by business. The idea behind viewing a system with a black box approach is to enhance the understanding of *what* the system does without knowing *how* it does it. Understanding the details of how something is accomplished does not necessarily help in redesigning that process or function. In fact, it may prove detrimental, since once you understand how something works, limitations or boundaries on what can be done arise.

Let's return to the payroll system example previously used in the software reengineering discussion. If information engineering techniques are used, instead of placing the boundaries of the system on existing applications, the boundaries may be expanded or contracted depending on the findings. Again, information engineering focuses on data used in the process, in this case, payroll. The emphasis on data rather than applications allows for a broader scope and can dramatically change how new software and systems will be developed. It still falls short, however, of looking at how the organization does business. It assumes that capturing data relevant to the way processes are currently done will provide breakthrough redesign efforts. Depending on the current processes in place, this may or may not be true. Analyzing the data rather than the applications allows for a more objective perspective of the problem or issue. However, it does not guarantee that major changes in processes will be the result of the analysis. The scope of the project must be broad enough to allow for cross-functional duplication of effort or redundancy to become apparent.

Project Phases

Information engineering projects can progress through several phases, which are similar to the phases of any project. Many vendor-supplied methodologies such as STRADIS follow a similar progression. This approach is a lot broader than software reengineering because it takes into account the business processes. In this regard, information engineering is similar to business reengineering with the starting point as the only difference. Information engineering starts after a clear mission has been determined by the organization. It looks strategically at the information systems and data within the organization. Information engineering's focal point is the data that is needed to accomplish a specific process. Business reengineering or BPR focuses on the business processes, questioning their existence and purpose. Business reengineering starts with reviewing the actual business the organization is in as well as defining its mission, regardless of technology. It takes a broader perspective of the processes under analysis. Issues which are not related to computer systems or information gathering are included in the scope of a reengineering project and, in many cases, are the focal point of that project. All projects, however, whether focused on information engineering or business reengineering follow the same steps: planning, analysis, design, and implementation (See Figure 2.1).

Planning is an integral part of any project. However, when considering reengineering your business (radically changing the way you do business), planning becomes even more critical. Most people can relate to attending a meeting where senior management presents some new ideas such as management by objective (MBO), total quality management (TQM), or even business reengineering. Everyone becomes enthusiastic about how they can achieve loftier goals and increase service and productivity. They leave the meeting euphoric, looking like the Dallas Cowboys taking the field at the Super Bowl. The feeling abounds that they can take on the world. However, a progress report a month later indicates that nothing has changed. No one knows exactly how to accomplish the sought-after outcome—increased produc-

Planning or Strategizing
Analysis **(understanding what needs to be done)**
Design **(determining how it will be accomplished)**
Construction or Implementation **(implementing the technology and/or changes)**

Figure 2.1 Phases of information engineering or business reengineering projects. Any project which follows the system development life cycle (SDLC) will contain certain phases or tasks. Depending on the methodology used, the name of tho phases may differ and where one phase ends and the other begins may differ; however, the four major sequences listed above occur in any project.

tivity with reduced costs. Embracing the concepts of reengineering without a plan to actually implement reengineering projects will produce this type of scenario.

This book provides an outline (Chapters 5 through 8) which can be adapted to develop a customized plan for implementing redesign projects. In order to provide a point of reference for reengineering projects and an overview of the phases of the system development life cycle (SDLC) outlined in Chapter 4, the phases of information engineering projects are discussed.

☑ *Planning*

The planning phase of information engineering is started at a high level of abstraction. In other words, there is not a great deal of detail uncovered at this time. This planning phase provides for assessing current technology and future needs. It allows an organization to determine which processes or functional areas should be analyzed first. A **functional area** is a unit in an organization which provides a specific function to the organization. It may or may not coincide with the traditional department structure. This phase also provides the ability to set the technological direction of the organization. For instance, if migrating from mainframe systems to client/server technology is a goal of the organization, it would be determined at this point in time. After the technology base for future development has been determined and a functional area or process is selected for further analysis, more detailed information needs to be accumulated.

☑ *Business Area Analysis*

After a functional area or process is targeted as a project, some form of analysis must occur. In Information Engineering this phase is called a business area analysis; in structured systems analysis it is called the analysis phase and would generate a feasibility study. No matter what term is used the outcome is the same.

- ◆ The scope of the system needs to be determined and general information gathered, in order to ascertain if further analysis is feasible.
- ◆ The details of what systems need to be developed to address the issues of the functional business areas is determined at this time.
- ◆ Time is spent ascertaining what needs to be accomplished rather than dwelling on how it will be done.

The black box approach is used at this time. In-depth knowledge of how computer systems work is not necessary at this time. After the analysis is completed the details must be gathered and the systems design work begins.

☑ *Design*

The systems are designed after all requirements are determined. Whether the project is an information engineering project, a systems analysis project, or a business reengineering project, there must be the ability to determine

- ◆ How a change will be implemented and must succeed.

♦ What the change should be which is determined in the analysis phase of the project.

Business reengineering projects or information engineering projects may split into several automated and manual processes to be further designed, and ultimately implemented by the organization.

☑ *Construction*

After the design of the system or systems is accomplished, the actual construction and implementation begins. This is the last development step of the process followed by an evaluation or assessment stage. Construction or implementation may mean programming applications for users or writing procedural manuals to change existing manual processes. Implementation ranges from manual to automate processes and encompasses the entire functional areas under consideration in the analysis phase.

Information engineering and software engineering follow the same logical progression toward developing an automated system; however, project phases or tasks may be grouped differently or the terminology may be different. This logical progression from planning to analysis, design, and implementation is based on the SDLC which is discussed in more detail in Chapter 4. In any case, the end result is the same. The major difference between information engineering and software engineering is the primary focus of the techniques. Systems analysis focuses primarily on the programs and flow of information with data as secondary, whereas information engineering focuses on the data primarily and the information flow second (see Figure 2.2).

Business Reengineering

Business Reengineering is the process that addresses the concerns of whether certain systems or processes should even exist. It extends beyond the scope of software reengineering in all its flavors, as well as information engineering.

Software Engineering	Focuses primarily on developing programming code to automate processes.
Information Engineering[1]	Focuses on developing automated systems. Primary emphasis is placed on analyzing the data requirements for either a specific system or the enterprise as a whole.
Modern Structured Systems Analysis	Focuses on developing automated systems, similar to information engineering. However, primary emphasis is placed on analyzing the processes within an organization to determine requirements, and the data is secondary.
Business Reengineering	Focuses on the business processes to determine how to redesign the processes automated or manual) to be more effective. Emphasis placed on the business needs first.

[1]Information engineering has been labeled as a technique and a methodology. It is viewed as a technique within the context of this book. It is a technique that nearly spans the entire system development life cycle (SDLC) and therefore is sometimes viewed as a methodology.

Figure 2.2   Techniques used to develop systems. Whether the system to be developed is a manual system, automated system, or a combination of both, various techniques may be applied to the project. The techniques listed are incorporated into various methodologies, both in-house developed methodologies and commercial ones such as STRADIS or Method 1. Each technique has its strengths and weaknesses. This chart identifies the focus of each of the techniques.

Various levels of business reengineering exist, from applying technology to an existing business process to redefining an organization's line of business. These various levels will be outlined later; the main levels are

♦   Technology application
♦   Work-flow analysis
♦   Business process redesign
♦   Business reengineering

Information engineering projects can span entire enterprises, from large-scope projects to application-specific, narrow ones. The same is true for business reengineering projects. In many instances the only reason a project is categorized as information engineering rather than business reengineering is the distinction of which department initiated the project. If a project originates from the Information Systems (IS) department or the equivalent department in a given organization, chances are it will be categorized as an information engineering project. Conversely, if the project originates from senior management and outside consultants are called in, chances are it will be categorized as a business reengineering project.

However, the perceived outcome can vary, depending on the way the project is classified. For instance, if a project is classified as an information engineering project, then the ability to make organizational changes, policy revisions, or any major functional changes to the way the organization operates will be difficult, if not impossible. By definition, information engineering projects focus on the data and subsequently the information flow, not the underlying business processes and procedures. Even though the project may suggest some organizational changes, and include procedural issues in its analysis, it may be difficult to proceed when the perception of the project scope by senior management is different from the project team's. Labeling the project as an information engineering project or business process redesign is important in ensuring that everyone's perception of the project is the same.

The scope is the main indicator to help ascertain what type of project is being undertaken, regardless of what it is categorized as. Most information engineering projects will fall into the realm of technology application or work-flow analysis; two varying degrees of business reengineering. Information engineering projects generally place emphasis on technology first and business functions and processes second.

Whether a project is defined as software engineering, information engineering, or business reengineering affects the perception of a project. Projects which focus on the computer systems versus the business processes and procedures should be classified either as software engineering, software reengineering, or information engineering. However, many projects which focus on the computer systems are labeled business process redesign or business reengineering projects. Many times this is because of internal political reasons. Funding may be available for business reengineering projects and not for enhancements to existing automated systems. An awareness of what each type of project represents regardless of what it is labeled is very useful information.

If a project focuses on the business processes or procedures, some of which may be automated, then the project is some type of a business reengineering project. It is important to understand the scope of the project, thereby better understanding the type of project it is. Understanding these differences and management's perception about each, will help determine what the project should be called and who should initiate it.

♦ Radically changing business processes, policies, and organization structure will result from business reengineering projects. These projects should be initiated by senior management or external consultants. Business process redesign and business reengineering projects fall within this category.
♦ Enhancements to existing information flows, automated or manual systems, or improved processes will result from information engineering projects. These projects should be initiated jointly between IS and the affected department management. Technology application and work-flow analysis projects fall within this category.

There are many different types of business reengineering projects. They can be defined by the scope of the project.

BUSINESS REENGINEERING PROJECTS DEFINED BY SCOPE

From the previous discussion it can be gathered that one of the ways to differentiate the type of project is through its scope.

♦ If a project begins by evaluating an existing computer application or system of applications, then it is probably a software reengineering project and certain tools and techniques can be applied.

♦ If focus is placed on the data or information necessary to complete the given function, then the project is probably an information engineering project and different tools and techniques should be applied.

♦ If the project begins by asking the question "Why are we even doing this?", then chances are it is some form of a business reengineering project and again, different tools and techniques apply.

In other words, there is no one set of tools, techniques, or methodologies that apply to all types of projects at all times.

The important thing to remember is that before you assign a group of people to a project, purchase tools, and train them in certain methodologies and techniques, the type of project to be undertaken should be clearly defined and understood. Just as a hammer is not an appropriate tool for measuring, the same holds true for the various tools available for reengineering projects. There are specific techniques and tools that are useful for work-flow analysis but not as effective when undertaking a business reengineering project. An analogy that has become prevalent in many business writings is

If the only tool you are familiar with is a hammer,
then every problem will look like a nail.

As a general rule, the broader the scope of a project, the more likelihood that innovation will occur. When the scope of a project is broad enough to allow various interpretations of the analysis, the opportunity for breakthrough results is increased. When a project is narrow in scope the results of the project must integrate with existing applications, systems, and procedures. By definition a narrow-scope project does not allow for major changes or innovations.

For example, when determining how to best utilize personnel within your company, if the scope of your investigation is limited to one department, your options are also limited. If a department has 30 people and five different functions, you can only redesign and reassign tasks within that scope. This limits the amount of change you can propose. However, if you look broader, for example to a division, there is more opportunity to redefine positions since redundancy and duplicate work may be uncovered. The wider the scope, the more options are available. The same concept holds true when analyzing information flows and business processes. The broader the scope, the more opportunity for change! Change, for change's sake is not desired. However, change, in order to eliminate redundancy, increase effectiveness, and reduce costs is a change for the better.

Business reengineering projects can be defined from the narrowest in scope, such as technology application, to the broadest scope, encompassing the entire organization (see Figure 2.3). The scope of a project is defined by the parameters placed around it. One way to define the scope of a project is to

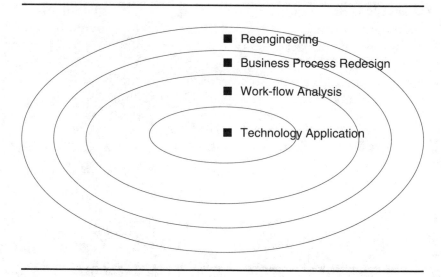

Figure 2.3   The scope of a project can be viewed as narrow to all-encompassing. Technology application projects have the narrowest scope as compared to reengineering projects which span the entire organization or a major portion of it. The scope of a project increases as more processes, people, and information are included in the project.

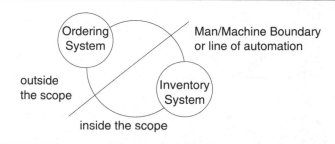

Figure 2.4 There must be a way to show what is within the scope of a project and what is outside the scope. The man/machine boundary is a systems analysis concept that allows systems designers to visually document what is within and outside the scope of automation. The concept can also be used, as in this illustration to depict what is within the scope of the project and what is outside the scope.

determine what processes and information or data are included in the analysis of the project. In other words, where is the line drawn? Systems analysts actually draw a line called a "man/machine boundary" on a data flow diagram, a modeling technique, to depict the scope of a project (see Figure 2.4). Whether a graphical illustration of the project and actual lines are drawn, the same concept needs to be applied. At some point the decision to include certain processes and data in a project must be made. Questions regarding what data and processes will be considered part of the system need to be asked.

For example, if a company centrally orders and maintains an inventory of office supplies for all of its departments, the scope of the system needs to be defined first. Should the ordering process which depletes the inventory be considered part of the system? Other issues related to scope include whether the ordering of inventory items from depleted stock will be part of the analysis. If so, will direct electronic ordering of new supplies or replenishing supplies through electronic data interchange (EDI) technology be part of the system. As this example illustrates, the scope of a project will directly affect success and also the level to which major changes and breakthroughs can be made.

There are very few organizations that have successfully

attempted global business reengineering—actually redefining the business they are in or the underlying fundamental processes in their business. Most of the existing success stories are applications of business process redesign or workflow analysis projects which were successfully implemented. These are projects of considerably less scope than business reengineering projects which change the entire organization and focus of the company. In some instances, business reengineering or changing the entire direction of a company is necessary. However, it is always useful to learn to walk before you run. Understanding the issues regarding business process redesign or business reengineering as well as the effect change has on individuals, as well as organizations, is imperative for success.

Technology Application

Technology application is the reengineering project with the narrowest scope. It usually focuses on one process within one department or a simple task shared by many departments. Applying an off-the-shelf software package to solve a specific business problem is an example of this type of project. For example, an electronic mail system may be installed to solve the problem of decreasing communications from distant offices to the central or home office. However, after installing electronic mail, the number of internal memorandums produced (electronic or paper) may continue to decrease. In effect the *method* of communication within the organization has changed from paper to electronic; however, the communication *process* has remained the same. Without addressing the underlying issue of why communications have decreased, technology was applied. Understanding the communication process within the organization is imperative to solving the problem of decreasing memorandums sent to the central office. Without the underlying communication process changing, substantive change will not occur. Substituting one technology for another will not solve the problem. In this scenario, the underlying business problem was the organizational hierarchy which stifled communications. The formal reporting structures and lines of command that originally stifled open communications still existed after the new technology (electronic mail) was installed. Therefore, a reengineering project encompassing a larger scope (internal communications) would be necessary to address that issue. As the name implies, technology application projects apply technologies to existing processes or tasks.

Work-Flow Analysis

Work-flow analysis focuses on processes which may be identified in technology application projects. The scope of this type of project is broader than technology application projects; however, it is still usually limited to a single process or task shared between a few departments. If changes are introduced that will affect the entire organization rather than only a few departments or areas, even if work-flow software will be applied, the project would fall under the category of a BPR project rather than a work-flow analysis project. Work-flow analysis projects may include applying technologies such as groupware or work-flow software; however, because manual processes will also change, and multiple departments are involved, the scope of the project is broader than technology application projects. Work-flow analysis attempts to either eliminate unnecessary steps or streamline steps within a specific process. Major changes to the way business is conducted is not addressed in this type of project, mainly because the scope is too narrow to allow radical changes to occur. However, productivity improvements can be obtained and the analysis gathered from this type of project can provide useful information for larger projects, such as BPR projects. The information gained from each of these different types of projects (technology application, work-flow analysis, BPR, and business reengineering) can be used as building blocks to the next project of larger scope. Figure 2.5 illustrates this example.

Business Process Redesign

Business process redesign focuses on the underlying business reasons why certain processes exist in their current form. As

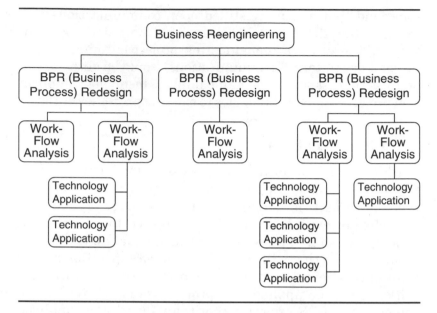

Figure 2.5 Technology applications projects can be viewed as building blocks to help define work-flow analysis projects. The same holds true for work flow analysis projects—they can be viewed as building blocks to business process redesign projects. The information obtained from smaller scope projects can be combined to help redesign processes at a more global scale.

stated earlier, electronic mail could be implemented as a technology application project; however, in order for the internal communication process to be enhanced, a BPR scope project would be necessary. The scope of a BPR project includes most, if not all, departments in the organization and focuses on processes which could provide major benefits to the organization through substantial changes in the way things are currently done. In the example of enhancing the communication process within an organization, the possible benefits would include reduced bureaucratic costs, as well as increased time between senior management's announcement of a direction and implementation of that direction. In order for these types of benefits to be achieved, changes may occur in organizational structures, promotion procedures, how risk-taking is dealt with, and compensation issues, as well as other areas.

BPR projects allow major changes to occur because the

scope of the project is broad enough. These projects, however, provide the opportunity for success because they are also narrow enough. This may sound contradictory; however, the scope of a project is critical to the project's success.

♦ The scope must be large enough to allow for change.
♦ It must be narrow enough to be manageable.

Reengineering projects, which address the basic functions of the business, are generally not successful because the staff is not initially aware of all the issues involved. BPR projects allow substantial change to occur within an organization, while providing experience for larger reengineering projects in the future.

Business Reengineering

Reengineering projects focus on the underlying functions of the organization. Reengineering, at this all-encompassing level, is generally thought of when the term reengineering is used. This text differentiates between various levels of reengineering projects according to scope—technology application, work-flow analysis, business process redesign, and business reengineering. This level of reengineering is what Mike Hammer alluded to in his initial *Harvard Review* article. However, much of the work done to date in reengineering is not being done at this all-encompassing level, but rather at the BPR or work-flow analysis scope. It is difficult to initiate changes so broad as to affect every department, and so drastic as to change the direction a company is moving in, without some experience to call upon. BPR projects provide this experience while providing ample opportunities for implementing changes which increase service, productivity, and ultimately profitability, while maintaining or reducing costs.

Conclusion

The scope of the project is an important aspect, especially when planning for implementation. The scope will determine the definition of the problem or the opportunity to change a given process by placing parameters around the

ope identifies what systems or processes will
part of the project, as well as what is defi-
he scope of the project. This is important to
e teams and time estimates are identified.
All projects (software reengineering, information engineering, and business reengineering) address the issue of scope
before any other steps can be accomplished. Without identifying the scope of a project, the actual problem or opportunity cannot be succinctly identified for resolution.

CHAPTER HIGHLIGHTS

✎ There are many different definitions of reengineering:
software reengineering, information engineering, and
business reengineering.
✎ Software reengineering focuses on the software rather
than the underlying business processes. There are several types of software reengineering projects such as:
   ◇ Restructuring code which focuses on the program code.
   ◇ Reverse engineering which starts by analyzing the
program code, but also extrapolates the design specifications from the code and looks at enhancing the
initial design before restructuring the code.
   ◇ Reengineering design specifications is similar to reverse engineering; however, it skips the step of analyzing the program code to extrapolate the design
specifications. This technique can only be used when
design specifications are available.
✎ The term software engineering defines a disciplined approach to software development. The term software
reengineering implies existing software is analyzed, design specifications are extrapolated, and new and improved software is written.
✎ Information engineering has been debated as to whether
it is a technique or a methodology. In either case, information engineering focuses on the data first and information flow second. It permits a project to encompass a
broader scope because of this focus, thus allowing more
changes to take place.

✎ Information engineering, just like structured systems analysis, follows the basic SDLC (System Development Life Cycle) approach to developing systems. The SDLC approach can be broken down in different phases and tasks; however, the major steps which exist in all projects that follow a SDLC methodology are:
◊ Planning
◊ Analysis (what)
◊ Design (how)
◊ Implementation (do it)

✎ Business reengineering projects focus on business processes, procedures, and organizational structures with a much broader scope than information engineering or software reengineering projects.

✎ The way in which a project is defined (business reengineering versus information engineering) can affect the outcome of the project because of the various perceptions of these terms.
◊ Information engineering projects are usually initiated by the IS department and focus on the data and information flows within or between departments. Major changes will probably not occur.
◊ Business reengineering projects are usually initiated by outside consultants, under the direction of senior management, and focus on policies, procedures, and organizational structures. Major changes will probably occur.

✎ Business reengineering projects can be defined by scope. The broader the scope, the more likely major changes within the organization will occur.

Technology Application (narrowest scope) This is the type of project which is more readily implemented. Replacing a typewriter with a computer, without changing the way work is done on the equipment, is an example of technology application.

Work-Flow Analysis (narrow scope) This is the type of project which can provide some substantial benefits to an organization. Major changes to the way business is done is not addressed; however, productivity improvements can occur at this level. Analyzing the work flow between an executive and secretary and customizing the work flow between them, probably using a computer, would provide increased benefit over just applying the technology to the situation.

Business Process Redesign (broad scope) This is the type of project with which most institutions that have implemented some type of business reengineering projects, have been successful. Following the same scenario of the typewriter and computer, BPR would address not only the work flow between the executive and the secretary, but also take into account why that work flow exists in the first place. Major changes to the way business is done can occur with this type of project. Questions such as, "Is the position of secretary necessary for each executive?" or "Should the position be combined with another function or changed altogether?" would be asked. Technology would be applied to this type of project, but only after the underlying business processes were analyzed and redesigned.

Business Reengineering (broadest scope) This is the type of project which most people think of when they hear the term business reengineering. Radical changes not only to the way business is done, but also to the organization's line of business are addressed at this level. In the typewriter/computer scenario, rather than determining whether executives and secretaries are performing the appropriate functions within the organization, an even broader scope of the problem is examined. For instance, the project may address why the company is in the business it is in. Outsourcing entire departments and fundamentally changing the mission of the institution may take place, possibly eliminating the need for a typewriter or some other technology for that task.

✎ It is recommended to walk before you run. Attempting a major business reengineering project without some practice on a smaller scale with a work-flow analysis or business process redesign project would be difficult to say the least.

Where Do You Begin?

Business process redesign projects are time-consuming and costly. Why then would organizations be willing to expend the required time and effort? Some of the reasons you would want to initiate or participate in a BPR project include:

- Increasing productivity, quality, and customer service.
- Reducing costs, errors, and redundant work.
- Cope with the "do more with less" syndrome present in today's business because of increased competition.

The promised results of increased productivity and decreased costs outweigh the time and effort expended. Before the time and effort are expended on any BPR project, commitment from senior management should be obtained. Senior management should be willing to implement the changes within their organizations. The concept of business process redesign is one that most people will agree is necessary. The idea of changing ineffective procedures and processes in order to reduce costs and increase efficiency and effectiveness seems logical to most people. However, the test of one's convictions comes at the point when tough decisions regarding implementing radical changes within an organization have to be made.

SELECTING A BPR PROJECT

Every organization can identify problems or opportunities for change. The best starting point is to locate current problems and concerns raised by various personnel. In order to have a broad perspective of the problems at any given institution, feedback should be obtained from all levels of management and staff. However, even without formal focus groups and surveys, most organizations can readily list some problems that need to be rectified. This type of information is a good starting point. If the information is not readily available, a senior staff meeting could generate some possible projects. The objective at this point is to identify a few possible projects which could be redesigned.

Determine the Type of Project You Have

How do you know if the project you have in mind is suitable as a business reengineering project? First you need to determine if the project you are contemplating really is some type of a reengineering project or is actually a software reengineering or information engineering project. If the project is not some type of reengineering project to begin with, as defined by scope, then even by following the guidelines in Chapters 5 through 8 major changes will not occur. It is important to realize the type of project you are dealing with when planning the project, in order to determine realistic outcomes.

♦ If the project appears to be focused on computer applications (software), it is probably either a software reengineering or information engineering project. In either case, you have two choices:
   1. Assign the project to either an internal IS department or outsource it to a company specializing in software development for resolution.
   2. Redefine the scope of the project to include underlying business processes and procedures and shift the focus from software and computer applications to business processes if the possible benefits to be de-

rived are great enough. Then the project can be evaluated as some type of business reengineering project.

♦ If the project appears to be focused on business processes, organizational structure, or procedures, it is some type of business reengineering project. The next step is to determine the project type based upon the initial scope.

If you determine the project's focus is on business processes rather than technology or data, then you need to ascertain the scope of the project in order to determine what type it is. If your project is narrow in scope and is classified as a work-flow analysis project, you can reasonably expect some productivity gains; however, major innovations and substantial improvement in quality or service with significant reduced costs will not occur. It is important to understand the range of outcomes available from each type of project in order to have reasonable expectations regarding the outcome of the BPR project. For instance, if you exchange the typewriter with a computer and do nothing else, don't expect major cost savings and productivity gains to occur.

♦ Business reengineering projects are broken down into four different types based on their scope.
   ◊ **Technology Application** (*narrowest scope, least amount of change*)
   ◊ **Work-Flow Analysis** (*narrow scope, some productivity improvement*)
   ◊ **BPR** (*broad scope, substantial change*)
   ◊ **Business Reengineering** (*broadest scope, greatest amount of change*)

You need to be flexible when implementing BPR concepts and techniques. As BPR was defined earlier, it is not a cookbook solution to business problem-solving. Even if you determine initially that a project is a work-flow analysis project, after the problem is studied further and new information is obtained, the scope may shift. This can cause the project to become either a technology application type of reengineering project if the scope narrows or a BPR type of reengineering project if the scope broadens.

Scope—A Critical Factor

During the steps completed when redesigning business processes you may have the feeling that you have addressed certain issues before. This is not *déjà vu*. You will continue to readdress certain issues throughout the project. Once you initially determine what type of project you are working on and what the scope is, you are not finished with those issues for the entire project—just for now. Scope will continually be addressed throughout the redesign process as more detailed information about the project is obtained. Flexibility is one of the keys to success when redesigning business processes.

In many ways redesigning a business process is like walking a tight rope between redefining the problem and scope of the project while moving forward with the project and continually redefining the scope to the point where no progress is made at all. You need to be sure to keep deadlines and outcomes in your mind and at some point put parameters around the project. This is one reason why defining the types of business reengineering projects by scope (technology application, work-flow analysis, business process redesign, business reengineering) helps you move forward with the project; it keeps parameters around the project. Once management and the team members agree upon what type of business reengineering project a specific endeavor is, if the scope changes to a point that it becomes another type of project, discussion will be needed before moving forward with the business reengineering project. In this way the "creeping scope" which many information systems analysts and programmers experience can be eliminated.

Creeping scope is a phenomenon that occurs when additional functionality is continually added throughout the entire project. In essence what is delivered as a final system is generally several times larger than the initial request. This can cause problems if deadlines need to be met and resources are limited. There are four variables that affect the outcome of a project:

- ◆ Time
- ◆ Resources (personnel and funding)

♦ Quality
♦ Scope

If any one of the four variables changes, one of the other three will have to compensate. In other words, if a project has a deadline (time) and a set budget and personnel allocated to it (resources), and the scope of the project becomes larger, either quality will suffer or the time frame will need to be adjusted and additional resources allocated. These project management variables exist for any type of project; however, they become extremely critical in business reengineering projects because the scope of the project can change, and usually does, between the time the project is initiated and the redesign phase. Figure 3.1 identifies the four phases of BPR projects as outlined in this book.

Remember, the success of the project is directly correlated to the scope of the project.

♦ If the scope is too large, you will not be able to make progress.
♦ If the scope is too narrow, there will not be enough opportunity to make changes that will be worth the investment of time and money.

BPR Phases	Tasks within phases
Planning	see Chapter 5
Redesign	see Chapter 6
Transition	see Chapter 7
Implementation	see Chapter 8

Figure 3.1 The Four Phases of Business Reengineering are recommended by the author as a way to implement BPR projects within an organization. The planning phase relates to identifying the project and determining whether the proposed project is in line with the goals of the institution. The redesign phase determines what the current process or system under investigation does and what it should do. The transition phase addresses how to implement the changes. The implementation phase is the portion of the project where the changes are implemented.

Even though a project's classification may change from work-flow analysis to business process redesign, or some other combination, it is important to initially identify the type of project both management and the project team members anticipate it to be. In other words, everyone involved in the project should have the same perception of the initial scope of the project and its associated outcomes. If a project team begins working on a project and they believe the scope of the project is a BPR project, while management views the project as either technology application or work-flow analysis, conflicts can arise. It is important that in the beginning everyone involved in a project has the same basic expectations regarding the outcome of the project—otherwise the success of the project is in jeopardy. If the first business reengineering project the institution attempts fails, there is the possibility that future initiatives will not be supported. Therefore, it is critical that a company's first business reengineering project be a success.

For example, one institution was reevaluating their internal ordering system and the project team itself had two different viewpoints regarding what the scope of the project was. The discussion to define what type of business reengineering project was being attempted never took place. The term BPR was used when discussing the internal ordering system project; however, the term itself was never defined and the scope was never fully understood by all parties involved. Half of the team was under the assumption that the project was a technology application type of reengineering project and was focusing on appropriate computer software solutions to the problem. The other half of the team was under the assumption that the project was a BPR project during which issues such as "Why are we even doing this process?" could be raised. The importance of defining the type of reengineering project lies in creating mutual understanding of the process and outcomes between all involved parties.

In order to eliminate the confusion experienced by this example BPR project team, agreement on what the expected outcome of the project is should be discussed and agreed upon by all involved individuals before the project begins.

The project previously described—the internal ordering system reengineering project—did not produce any major changes. New technology was simply applied to the existing processes. This was also the first business reengineering project the company attempted. Needless to say, there have been no further business reengineering initiatives contemplated at this particular institution. Their first encounter with business reengineering was not successful; therefore, allocating additional resources to this type of endeavor was deemed futile. As a rule of thumb, if there is confusion about the scope of the project or the expected outcomes, the narrower the scope, the option of less change will prevail.

Strive for Initial Success

The success of the first BPR project undertaken by an organization is critical, as the previous example illustrates. People are resistant to change and will be watching to see what happens when a concerted effort to radically change a portion of the business is attempted. Success of the first BPR project will encourage skeptical individuals to look more closely at BPR and will not allow those firmly against change any ammunition. Of course, you want every project to succeed. However, the first project undertaken by an organization will be the most difficult because not only do you have the issues of the project itself to work on while learning new techniques and skills in order to complete the project, but also, the entire organization is closely watching the project to determine the possible benefit of reengineering to the organization as a whole.

Commitment to BPR is more than accepting the ideas and the concepts; it is radically changing processes within the company which may not be politically or culturally supported within the current organizational infrastructure. Every organization has its own political and cultural environment which places boundaries or borders around what is acceptable and what is not within that organization. Every institution has its "sacred cows," those departments or functions which are off limits to change. Acknowledging and identifying where those sacred cows exist in different organizations is critical to the success of the project.

If an initial business reengineering project attempted at an institution threatened a sacred cow department or function, the project would fail. Universities and colleges are prime examples of institutions that have departments deemed as sacred cows; to threaten their existence, or even change the way things are done or change the reporting structures is taboo. Each institution will have different sacred cows; for example:

♦ Entire departments
♦ Specific functions or jobs within departments
♦ Certain computer applications that were written internally
♦ Procedures or forms which have been developed and maintained internally

The rational for any of these sacred cows is not logical but political and cultural. Since each organization has its own history, it is difficult to understand why resistance to change will be greater in certain areas of the organization without understanding that history. Understanding and identifying the sacred cows within your institution will help you select an initial business reengineering project that does not include a sacred cow department or function. Maybe the departments or functions being protected need to be evaluated; however, this is not the type of project you want to initially undertake. After successful BPR projects have been completed, projects including institutional sacred cows can be contemplated.

Change is difficult not only for individuals, but for organizations as a whole. When major change is introduced into an organization, the current infrastructure is threatened. It is safer to do nothing than to champion dramatic change. Inertia is a powerful force to overcome. It is more difficult for an organization to apply BPR concepts to its existing processes if the personnel have been with the organization for a long time or if there is a great deal of history and culture to overcome. Precedence has been set and people have become comfortable with the way things are done. Additional support and encouragement may be necessary if the personnel involved in radical changes have been with the organization a long time. Follow-up and follow-through are major factors in any project, especially in business process redesign projects where change is involved.

Selecting Initial BPR Projects

Carefully identifying and selecting which projects will undergo redesign is imperative for success. Initial BPR projects undertaken by an organization should have the following characteristics:

◆ Top management commitment
◆ Scope determination and definition
◆ Senior management priority
◆ Significant organizational benefits
◆ Key management participation

Business reengineering can occur at different levels in the organization simultaneously. Less drastic changes from technology application or work-flow analysis reengineering types of projects with a limited scope, usually involving a single department, can occur while more global projects contemplating radical changes in the way business is done are being completed. Not all potential projects are candidates for BPR redesign or change. Some projects, because of their scope, may be well suited for narrower scope type projects such as work-flow analysis and automation efforts. How do you determine what project would be suitable for applying process redesign concepts and techniques? The scope of a project is a critical factor in determining its suitability as an initial BPR project within an organization. The proverbial deck should be stacked for the first business process redesign project undertaken by any organization: Choose a project which is positioned for success. Determining which projects will undergo the effort involved in redesign projects is critical to the success of implementing change within an organization. Some issues to consider when selecting an initial BPR project include:

◆ If the project is too small or does not have the ability to provide substantial benefit to the organization, it should not be the first redesign project undertaken.

◆ Processes which only affect one department should not generally be the first redesign project under taken. The limited scope will also mean limited impact of the redesign process.

◆ Many of the organizations who have been polled as having undergone BPR projects have indicated the majority of failures were caused by taking on large and complex projects initially.

◆ The time frame for the initial BPR project is important. The project should be completed within six months to a year in order to illustrate initial success quickly.

◆ The focus of a BPR project in which departmental managers will be spending their time should involve a more global view of the organization. The process selected for an initial BPR project should span several departments, but not the entire organization.

◆ The big picture of how a contemplated change fits into the overall structure of the organization should be clearly understood. In this manner, it can be determined if the process is one that would lend itself to a successful BPR undertaking.

◆ In some instances a sequence of events or small projects can become part of a larger BPR project that will involve major changes. For example, prior to redesigning processes, technology may be applied to a current process in order to free some of the staff's time to look at making major changes. Therefore, a technology application project may precede a BPR project.

Many techniques and issues are involved in redesigning processes—remember, the purpose is not to automate existing processes. If existing processes are being automated,

◆ either the processes should have been reviewed and deemed effective by the organization, or

◆ the automation should be viewed as a first step to free up some time to allow the staff time to critically look at their current business processes and procedures.

The participants of the BPR project will need to learn new skills and techniques. They will also need to become knowledgeable in group dynamics, team participation, and team building. This initial learning will take time during the first few projects undertaken. A learning curve exists for the individuals assigned to the first redesign project team. A time commitment is also required from team members. Many of the team members on BPR projects will be supervisors and managers involved with the day-to-day operation of the business. They can only spend so much time away from their regular duties.

Culture—An Issue to Consider

Implementing business process redesign projects requires changing the organization's culture—to allow acceptance of change to take root. Most organizations which have any type of longevity have had success with their past procedures. Thus, tradition and history have proven their strategies successful. Those organizations will be reluctant to change. Just because past processes were effective does not mean they will continue to be successful. Because the environment in which business operates is changing, many organizations which have enjoyed success throughout the years are struggling to keep their share of the market. Competition is fiercer, technology is changing more rapidly, and global trade and business is increasing at an accelerated pace. What has been successful for businesses in the past may prove detrimental in such a fast-paced, changing environment. Tradition, bureaucracy, and huge conglomerates with many layers of management cannot keep pace with their smaller, more agile competitors.

Not all redesign efforts, especially smaller scope workflow projects, can be completed with central resources. The expected benefits derived from projects with narrower scopes may not outweigh the time and resources required. Indi-

viduals within departments need to understand reengineering concepts in order to make changes within their departments. Many processes are within the control of a
particular office or department. People should understand
reengineering concepts well enough to apply them to processes within their control. In order to facilitate this, the
organizational culture must encourage risk-taking. People
must be secure in the notion that it's all right to try new
things, to do things differently. Not all changes will be effective. However, without encouraging change, there is likely
to be none. How can these minor changes take place? In
Chapter 1, the issue of how future management is trained
also addressed this concern. It is an issue that cannot be
avoided if successful business reengineering is to take place.

Sending staff to workshops on reengineering or business
process redesign will provide them with an understanding
of the concepts; however, it will not motivate them to look
within their own sphere of influence to make minor changes.
Changes must occur at all levels of the company in order to
create a truly dynamic organization which can adapt to the
changing world around it. By combining just-in-time (JIT)
training techniques with the business process redesign
projects, both objectives can be met. The individuals participating in the BPR project will not only be contributing to
global reengineering projects, but will also learn the techniques and methods necessary to redesign processes within
their own departments. For example, managers participating in redesign projects can learn skills to take back to their
departments. By using mapping or some other technique
learned by participation in an interdepartmental BPR
project, managers can eliminate non-value added steps or
redesign the flow of work within their jurisdictions. If they
are committing their time to business reengineering projects
there should be some payback for them.

Learning reengineering concepts and techniques, managers can evaluate existing as well as new processes and
eliminate inefficiencies, thereby continually improving their
function within the organization. The idea of changing pro-

cesses and doing things better, which is the underlying concept behind BPR projects, should be done at multiple levels within an organization. Departments should be investigating ways to eliminate unnecessary steps within their processes, and organizations as a whole should be investigating ways to eliminate redundant effort between departments and streamline business processes at an interdepartmental level. In order for an organization to take advantage of BPR concepts, the idea of continually assessing and improving how things are done should become part of the organization's culture.

Selecting Future BPR Projects

Subsequent BPR projects can have a larger scope than the first few projects undertaken. The more narrower scope projects undertaken, the more initial information on estimating time and resources needed is available to estimate broader scope projects. Figure 2.5 illustrates the concept of building upon previous experiences—leveraging the knowledge obtained from narrower scope projects before moving onto broader scope projects. Personnel involved in these narrower scope initiatives will become more proficient in reengineering concepts and techniques.

In most cases, IS staff will be involved in some portion of BPR projects since technology is usually an enabler, allowing changes to occur. IS staff on the team have a tendency to recommend automating existing processes, emphasizing that simply automating a process will provide enough benefits and provide the required justification. Being aware of these tendencies can help you understand the different viewpoints that different team members will bring to the project. However, the process itself must be evaluated and analyzed before automation is even brought up as an issue unless the automation is a stepping stone for major changes.

The Software Engineering Institute (SEI) of Carnegie Mellon University has developed a methodology for classifying an organization's "software process maturity" into five levels. (Rubin 1993) The same logic sequence of evolution can be applied to BPR projects.

◆ *First time project undertaken*
   In the first level of SEI's model, the initial project is undertaken. If the project is the first experience for anyone in the organization, it is a learning experience. Guidelines, such as those presented in Chapters 5 through 8 of this book, are detailed and customized for the organization during this initial level.

◆ *Able to repeat project*
   When the guidelines are customized into specific steps that the organization can repeat, the second level of maturity in the model is reached (see Figure 3.2). When the steps or tasks for redesigning business processes

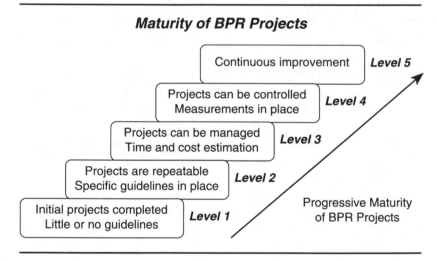

Maturity of BPR Projects

Figure 3.2 The Software Engineering Institute (SEI) of Carnegie Mellon University developed a model related to the maturity of the software development process. The underlying concepts provide the basis for the maturity of BPR projects depicted here. The initial BPR project undertaken by an organization would be at level 1, unless they were able to leverage outside consultants, whereby they may begin at level 2. However, several projects will have to be undertaken before accurate time and cost estimates are available. The goal is that eventually how BPR projects are undertaken within an organization is continually improved and streamlined (level 5).

have been defined and repeated, level two has been attained. The BPR process at this stage could be repeated by others in the company not necessarily on the first project team by following the tasks previously identified. However, it would be best to distribute some of the initial BPR project team members to subsequent projects in order to leverage the knowledge they've gained from working through the steps necessary to redesign business processes previously. This would also facilitate the objective of providing JIT training to the members of subsequent BPR projects. Team members from the first project can serve as trainers to those members on subsequent projects. The best way to truly understand something is to teach it. Figure 3.3 illustrates how this concept of JIT training can be built into the BPR project.

♦ *Managing the projects*
The next level in the model identifies managing the guidelines or steps of a redesign process. Redesigning processes within an organization is a process in itself that can be managed and controlled. In other words, once the guidelines for a BPR project have been defined, those guidelines or steps can then be managed and coordinated. At this point, not only can you repeat the steps completed in an initial BPR project, but you can also manage and estimate costs and completion dates for future projects more effectively. At this time you would be able to estimate more accurately the length of a BPR project based on its scope. There could be multiple BPR projects managed simultaneously within the organization.

♦ *Measuring and controlling the projects*
After a process can be managed, it can be controlled. Feedback and quality control issues can be built into the BPR process itself. Just as developing software applications is a process controlled through methodologies built upon the SDLC, developing redesigned processes needs some type of methodology to allow for repeatable success. The guidelines provided in Chapters 5 through 8 provide the outline of a methodology which can be cus-

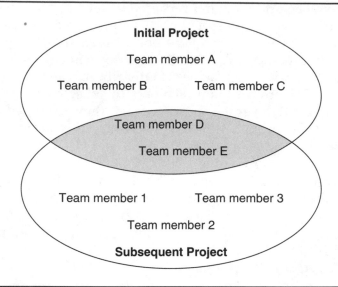

Figure 3.3 Building JIT (Just-in-Time) training into BPR projects. This diagram graphically depicts the relationship between the members of an initial BPR project and a subsequent project. By overlapping team members the function of redesigning business processes can be repeated sooner. In the example, team members D and E learned a great deal by working on the initial project. They would become team members of the subsequent project and adopt the role of not only participant, but also trainer, helping team members 1, 2, and 3 understand the phases of the BPR project and the techniques to help facilitate successful completion of the project. Team members D and E also benefit, because they need to fully understand the concepts and techniques involved in business process redesign in order to teach those skills and concepts to the new team members.

The initial project group would contain team members (A, B, C, D, and E). The subsequent project group would contain team members (1, 2, 3, D, and E).

tomized by individual organizations and eventually managed and controlled.

♦ *Continuous improvement*
Once a process can be repeated, managed, and controlled it can then be monitored for continuous improvement. BPR projects follow certain steps or guidelines—planning, redesign, transition, and implementation. Once the tasks that comprise each of these phases are identified, docu-

mented, and repeatable the foundation is in place to improve the guidelines for redesigning processes. Continuous improvement cannot occur until the guidelines have been defined, refined, documented, and tested in order to determine where improvement could be made. This is a vital reason why you need to document the steps or methodology of your redesign process. This book provides you with the phases and some guidelines for each of those phases identified; however, the guidelines provided here will need to be refined and tested in your specific environment.

TEAM BUILDING—A WELCOME SIDE EFFECT

Being part of a BPR team can provide several benefits for individual team members. Not only will team members learn about BPR techniques and methods, but also they will build relationships with other individuals in different departments. They should have a better perspective of how the processes within their departments affect other areas within the organization. As organizations move toward flatter structures, and remove hierarchies, it is imperative that middle managers and administrative personnel are able to work in cross-functional teams. Participating as a team member on BPR projects allows this to take place. Team members will also be able to apply some of the concepts they learn while participating in a BPR project within their own departments.

Not all team members should be selected by senior management during the planning phase. The key roles, such as project leader and management representatives from the appropriate departments should be assigned at this time. However, any additional team members required should be assigned by the initial BPR project team members themselves during the beginning of the redesign phase. The BPR project team, should be empowered to assign additional team members as necessary. In many instances, portions of the BPR project team will fluctuate throughout the project. Certain people will be required during different phases of the

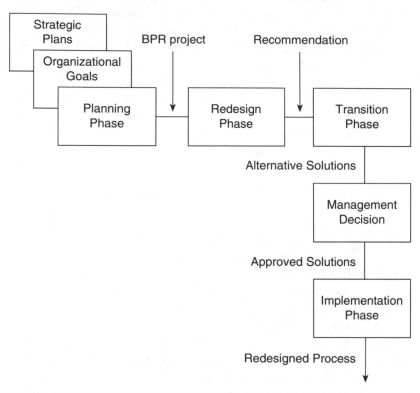

Figure 3.4 The four phases of a BPR project, as recommended in this book, consist of the Planning Phase, the Redesign Phase, the Transition Phase, and the Implementation Phase. Each phase has an outcome which is used by subsequent phases. This sequence of events is noted using mapping techniques to graphically depict the relationship. This relationship could have also been depicted using a data flow diagram.

project because of their skill set. (See Figure 3.4 which outlines the phases of a BPR project.)

Information systems professionals or outside technical consultants may participate in the transition phase to determine what types of technologies could enable proposed changes in order to determine feasibility. They may not be required to participate in further phases of the project. By allowing team membership to fluctuate, you can take advantage of the internal and external expertise required to make the project a success without requiring an expert's commitment throughout the entire project.

Some team members will remain static throughout the entire project, while others will come and go depending on the focus of the various phases. The fluctuation of team members provides an environment where new ideas may be sparked by new team members or when certain technologies are introduced as a possible solution to the redesign. This may occur either during the redesign or transition phase.

PHASES OF BPR PROJECTS

Any project undertaken must include a plan. This plan must fit into the overall goals of the organization. In the first phase of a business reengineering project (planning phase), the projects undertaken must correspond to the goals of the organization. Senior management should determine which projects will undergo business process redesign efforts. You wouldn't take a trip without a road map and a planned route. A builder wouldn't dream of building a house without a blueprint. A BPR project should not be contemplated without a methodology or plan for accomplishing the project. All BPR projects, regardless of the company implementing the business process redesign concepts, have the same major phases. First, determination of the focus and scope of the project is necessary, followed by the redesign phase, transition phase, and implementation. The phases are identified at this point, along with some issues related to each phase. However, a detailed discussion of each phase and guidelines to help you determine how to implement each phase can be found in Chapters 5 through 8.

Planning Phase

The planning phase (Chapter 5), which is the first phase of any BPR project, has several issues that need to be addressed before you can move on to actually redesign a process.

◆ Senior management agreement on the project selected
◆ Definition of project scope
◆ Identification of feasibility issues, including technical, economical, and political factors
◆ Determination and quantification of benefits when possible
◆ Assignment of team members
◆ Synchronization of organizational goals and projects
◆ Determination of objectives (Team building may be a serendipitous benefit of a BPR project.)

Redesign Phase

After an initial project has been identified, the second of the four recommended BPR project phases needs to be accomplished. (The redesign phase will be discussed in detail in Chapter 6.)

The major focus of this phase is to determine *what* the problem is. Many times the initial problem identified in the planning phase is actually a symptom rather than a problem. Therefore, the scope of a project may change once it has entered the redesign phase. This phase is similar to the analysis phase in methodologies adhering to structured analysis or information engineering techniques. The redesign phase incorporates the following:

◆ Look at the big picture and how the system under consideration fits into the other systems within the organization.
◆ Develop breakthrough thinking—break out of the old "this is the way we have always done it" mold.
◆ Determine what problem or opportunity is being addressed and redesign the processes accordingly.
◆ Study the existing system only enough to provide understanding without limiting breakthrough thinking.
◆ Recommend what the new system should do; not *how* it will be accomplished.
◆ Recommend any consultants or internal experts required during the transition phase of the project.

Transition Phase

Next you need to determine *how* you will implement this change within your particular organization—the transitional phase (Chapter 7). This phase takes the recommendations generated from the previous phase and looks at alternative ways the recommendations could be implemented. Assessing technology and its application to the various business processes under scrutiny is done at this time. During this phase the best solution will be designed. If computer systems are part of the recommended implementation, then the required applications programs will be identified at this time, as well as the computer platforms which will run the software. Technical issues regarding how the system will be implemented, even if the system is completely manual, are addressed during the transitional phase. The term implies the function of this phase—transitioning between the conceptual redesign and implementing the changes. This phase's tasks include the following:

♦ Determine which technologies could be applied to the redesigned processes.
♦ Determine how the redesign will physically be implemented.
♦ Recommend any technologies, personnel, or consultants required during implementation.
♦ Develop a general implementation plan for the next phase. Specific details will be added to the plan during the beginning of the implementation phase.

Implementation Phase

Many projects have failed at the implementation phase (Chapter 8) because of the difficulty of actually making changes and sticking to them. Inertia must be addressed and overcome during this phase of the project. Many times a situation is analyzed and talked about, meetings are scheduled, and maybe even teams are set up to investigate the situation, but nothing is ever implemented. The implementation phase is the portion of the BPR project when whatever changes are proposed are actually implemented. Tasks completed during this phase include:

- ◆ Write computer programs or integrate systems.
- ◆ Train end users in skills and concepts.
- ◆ Document changes, both manual and automated.
- ◆ Introduce changes to the organization.
- ◆ Develop an assessment plan.

CONSULTANT'S ROLE

There are some benefits, as well as drawbacks, for involving external consultants in your business reengineering efforts. Turning over your entire business reengineering project to an external consulting firm would not be the best choice, but neither would trying to do the entire process on your own, especially, the first time. The optimum involvement from consultants is somewhere in the middle. The major concern is selecting the right type of consultant. You want a consultant who is willing to train your staff and work with them using JIT training principals in order for you to duplicate their work. Some tasks which an external consultant can perform for you include:

- ◆ Review business reengineering plans and assess how they support the organization's mission.
- ◆ Review the information technology (IT) plan and ascertain whether this along with the business reengineering plan and the mission of the organization are synchronized.
- ◆ Review or develop business reengineering project plans— customize the guidelines provided here for your specific institution.
- ◆ Conduct initial focus groups to discuss business reengineering and familiarize senior management with concepts.
- ◆ Provide advice at various phases of the BPR project.
- ◆ Assess the environment to determine how to develop a business reengineering plan.

♦ Review recommended solutions along with background material in order to raise any questions and alleviate potential problems before implementation.

External consultants can bring expertise and objectivity to a project. However, you must be aware that they can bring hidden agendas. It is imperative that you ascertain whether the consultant is affiliated with any particular software or hardware vendor in order to alleviate the possibility of any conflict of interest. Most consultants are reputable; however, there have been instances when the desire to implement a leading-edge technology has blurred their ability to provide the best solution for the client. In a business reengineering project, technology should be applied only when it can enable the proposed change to occur more readily—it should not drive the change.

Beware of the consultant who can assess your needs in a day and recommend a technical solution to your problem One company hired an external consultant to solve its need for statistical information on prospective clients. The firm needed to be able to determine which portions of their marketing plan were most effective in order to ascertain which initiatives they should continue. The consultant recommended a solution which was considerably more expensive and would take longer to implement than the solution the company's internal IS staff recommended. However, the consultant's recommendation was based on employing leading-edge technology. The actual business process was not even analyzed, but a technical solution was identified. One practice that will ensure you don't spend money on solutions you don't need is to get a second opinion. Having another consultant review the recommendations is a way to uncover hidden agendas and ensure that you are getting the best consulting services possible.

Not all consultants are able to bridge the gap between understanding business processes and knowledgeability about technology. Using the model of changing team members at different phases of the project, you can use consultants with technical expertise when needed and those with business knowledge or redesign expertise at different times during the project. In this manner you can leverage not only your internal staff, but the funds you expend for external consulting advice as well.

CHAPTER HIGHLIGHTS

✎ Planning is an important phase of any project, especially a business process redesign project. Whether the scope of the project is limited and involves technology application, or broad and encompasses the entire organization through a reengineering project, planning should be the first step. Part of planning is concerned with shaping the subsequent phases of the project and defining specifics such as scope and feasibility.

✎ Senior management must determine which processes should even be investigated for possible redesign. The processes that are selected should relate directly to the strategic plans or overall goals of the organization. Time and effort should not be spent on redesigning processes which the organization as a whole does not deem critical. For example, suppose part of the strategic plan of an organization specified that the company's direction was to enhance its retail operations and eliminate its mail order operation over a period of five years. If a redesign project was suggested to look at the mail order operation, senior management must determine whether they want to redesign this process given the strategic direction indicated, before any time and resources are expended. These are the types of issues that must be completed before planning issues such as scope, feasibility, and team identification are addressed for specific projects.

✎ The first project undertaken should be chosen not only for its support of the strategic plan for the organization, but also for its ability to succeed. A BPR project should not be initially undertaken if there are any political issues involved with it.

✎ The first BPR project should also have a relatively short time frame. It should be completed within six months to a year so that a success can be celebrated within this time frame. If an initial BPR project is selected which takes three or more years, it is difficult for senior management to approve funding for additional BPR projects, since the outcome of the first project has not been ascertained. Also, it is difficult for staff to become excited about changes that may not be seen for several years. The time frame is an important aspect when planning the initial projects.

✎ The culture of an organization is an important factor to take into consideration when developing a BPR project plan. If an organization's culture does not support risk-taking, and the existing culture is strong, bringing in an outside consultant to assist with the first BPR project will help promote reengineering initiatives in general and facilitate change within the culture. Internal personnel will not be willing to champion a BPR project, if the consequences are they may lose their job if they don't succeed.

✎ Team building may be a serendipitous benefit of BPR projects. As organizations move toward a flatter organizational structure, the ability to work in teams on specific projects is a necessary skill, whether it is a BPR project or any other type of project within the organization.

✎ The phases of a BPR project are:
Planning (Is it worth investigating and improving?)
Redesign (What do we need to do?)
Transition (How do we do it?)
Implementation (Do it!)

✎ Consultants can provide valuable information and an objective viewpoint. However, you want to retain control of the project and use external consultants at key points in the process and to help develop plans. Consultants can also provide second opinions regarding recommendations. Many times this type of review work can be done off site (sending the documentation to the consultant's office) and communicating via telephone. This keeps the cost of the review down and still enables you to have any questions you need answered before proceeding with the project.

4

How Do You Approach the Problem?

Once you have chosen a project what do you do next? Before you can plan how to address the issue you need to be sure you are addressing the appropriate issue. Determine whether the project identified is actually a problem or an advantageous opportunity rather than a symptom of a problem.

PROBLEM OR OPPORTUNITY?

Many systems have been developed which did not solve any problem or take advantage of any new opportunity.

This statement may seem ludicrous at first glance. Who would spend time and money to implement a new computer system or change the policies and procedures in an organization without either resolving a problem or taking advantage of an opportunity? Of course, no one would intentionally invest time and money for no reason. They would assume that a problem or opportunity has been succinctly and accurately identified to begin with before any changes are made. Unfortunately, many solutions have actually remedied symptoms rather than solved problems. How can you tell whether you have properly identified the problem or opportunity?

Various systems analysis methodologies and business problem-solving methodologies attempt to distinguish between a problem and an opportunity. It is more important, however, to determine that a problem or opportunity is accurately defined than to differentiate whether it should be classified as a problem or opportunity. Therefore, defining exactly what you perceive the problem or opportunity to be should be your main concern.

Opportunity for Change

One organization's problem may be another organization's opportunity. As stated earlier, it is more important to resolve the issue rather than try to determine whether an issue should be categorized as a problem or opportunity. Both problems and opportunities would be addressed in the same way, either through a customized approach using the SDLC (System Development Life Cycle), a generic business problem-solving model, or a combination of the two as presented in this book. However, there are certain situations which provide an ideal opportunity for applying business process redesign concepts, namely, downsizing and mergers or acquisitions.

Downsizing

A common trend today is downsizing or, as some allude to the trend, rightsizing. The idea behind this trend is to migrate from large mainframe systems to networked client/server-based computing or mini-computer networked systems. Books have been written on the pros and cons of this trend. The benefits/advantages of downsizing will not be addressed here. As it relates to business process redesign, the decision to downsize for whatever reasons is an opportunity to look at the way you do business. The computer systems that originally resided on the mainframe and the manual procedures associated with them should be reevaluated.

In many cases legacy systems (outdated mainframe systems) should not be migrated to client/server technology the way they are currently designed. Hardware and software limitations were built into the programs at the time they were developed. These built-in limitations affected the business processes associated with them. Additional manual steps may have been introduced to compensate for these limitations. For example, at one time programs needed to be written in such a way that portions of the program could be swapped back and forth between memory and storage since there was a 64K RAM (random access memory) limitation. The program logic was designed around the limitation of the computing power, but was not the most efficient with respect to personnel. There are computer programming tools and compilers that will allow you to port (move your applications with the logic intact) to a new platform. However, if you simply do this, have you accomplished any long-term benefits? You have moved logic developed around hardware limitations which in most instances is not user-friendly or efficient from a personnel standpoint.

The hardware and computing infrastructure in place at your organization is only as useful as the applications and systems residing on it. If you install the latest hardware and port outdated applications programs to it, you have not accomplished any major benefits (see Figure 4.1). You may

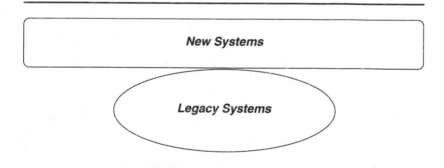

Figure 4.1 New systems should be built upon a solid foundation, not one that is unstable. Redesigned processes or new systems need to be built upon effective processes just as a building must be constructed on a solid foundation. Legacy systems which were designed around outdated technologies and associated limitations should not be the foundation for new systems. Building new systems on top of legacy systems is like building a house on an unstable foundation.

have saved maintenance costs on the old equipment, but productivity has not been increased. Also, how your employees interact with the computer systems is a key area of potential productivity improvement. Windows technology allows employees to be more productive. If your downsizing effort includes migrating existing COBOL or other third-generation programming languages rather than taking advantage of the new technologies, an opportunity for major improvement is missed.

Mergers and Acquisitions

Headlines in newspaper and trade journals constantly illustrate that companies are continually merging or being acquired. When this happens the acquiring company often retains its computer systems or the two merging companies choose one of the computer systems to handle the newly formed organization. This may be an excellent opportunity for redesigning processes and systems which otherwise would be missed. Instead of choosing one computer system over the other, why not take the opportunity to combine the best of both? Determine the strengths and weaknesses of each computer system and analyze the procedures used. By expanding the scope beyond the computer system to include personnel and procedures, as well as evaluating the logic of both computer systems, a starting point for a redesign project emerges. Take advantage of opportunities like this to determine what you are trying to accomplish and reassess your current processes. Remember, many systems have been developed which did not solve any problems or take advantage of any new opportunities. You want to be sure you do not migrate this type of system to your new platform or choose this type of system when merging operations.

PROBLEM OR SYMPTOM?

The main concern that must be addressed is whether or not you are solving the problem or just a symptom of the problem. The following scenario provides an excellent business example of this idea. A new departmental manager was assessing the tasks and assignments his employees were working on. After talking with several of them, he became aware of the fact that portions of their positions were not applicable to the work the department was intended to do. One person was not only performing administrative tasks for his purchasing department, but was also configuring computer systems. At first glance, the problem seemed to be that the departmental structure and consequently the positions within that department were not accurately defined. However, after talking with other departmental managers he discovered that the problem existed in other departments. At this point in the problem-solving process, he began to question whether the problem was actually the assignment of tasks to individuals, as he originally thought. After delving deeper it became apparent to him that the disjointed tasks assigned to individuals were really symptoms of a more global problem. Within this particular organization, salary was based upon job classifications, and job classifications were based upon tasks performed. Some individuals who were stellar employees could not be rewarded because they had reached the top of their specific classification and associated pay scale. Therefore, in order to reward these stellar employees, new tasks, and consequently new classifications were created. As a result individuals held titles and associated responsibilities that did not necessarily relate to their primary job function. The disjointed task assignments that evolved were not the problem but a symptom of an inadequate personnel/reward system. Sometimes it is not easy to see the problem if you are too close to it. Many times you can become wrapped up in trying to solve a problem that you never take the time to step back and ask yourself if what you are solving is really a problem or simply a symptom of a larger problem.

PROBLEM-SOLVING APPROACH

Scope—How It Applies to Defining the Problem

The definition of the problem will vary depending on the project scope. As the scope of the project changes, so does the problem. The example of job tasks previously described involved a scope issue. If the scope of the project, as the manager defined it, remained within his department, he would never have become aware that the problem existed outside his department. Therefore, the ability to determine that disjointed task assignments were a symptom rather than a problem, would not have become apparent. The scope of a project is directly correlated to the ability to define the actual problem. If you do not expand the scope large enough, at least to determine patterns, you may not be able to define the actual problem. Eventually the scope of the project may need to be reduced in order to manage the project; however, initially you need to look as broadly as possible in order to ensure you are solving the problem rather than a symptom.

What Is the Problem?

Business problem-solving is the same as any other type of problem-solving. Before any problem can be resolved, it must be identified and fully understood. Problem-solving first involves identifying and articulating the problem. If you can't explain what the problem is, it hasn't been clarified enough for action. Once the actual problem has been identified, however, there is another important question that requires consideration: "Is it worth solving?" Here the individual's business expertise is important. An organization cannot afford to solve every problem it has identified. If the identified problem is not linked to the corporate mission of the organization, valuable resources should not be allocated for its resolution. However, before that decision is made, an investigation should be made to determine if the problem under consideration is really a problem or a symptom of a larger problem. The following five steps outline decision-making when identifying whether a problem should be resolved.

♦ Identify and articulate the problem.
♦ Determine if the problem is linked with the organization's mission and goals.

◆ Ensure that the problem is a problem and not a symptom of a larger problem.
◆ Decide how to resolve the problem.
◆ Determine if resolving the problem will affect other areas of the organization.

How Should the Problem Be Solved?

The problem-solving process includes management's decision as to whether a problem will be resolved through reengineering efforts, traditional information systems development, reallocation of resources, or elimination of the function and therefore the problem. All problems are not resolved through reengineering efforts. The concepts of business process redesign and reengineering, however, can and should be used for problem resolution. Continuous assessment of how you do business and judging your procedures not only on efficiency, but also on effectiveness is part of the problem-solving process. If, for example, a problem is resolved by reallocating resources, has the problem really been resolved or has another problem been created?

What Is the Impact of Solving the Problem?

The organization is a system comprised of subsystems, which is analogous to the subsystems within the human body. Organizations consist of multiple subsystems such as finance, production, marketing, and personnel to name a few. Humans consist of multiple subsystems also, such as the circulatory, digestive, and respiratory systems. Just as your digestive system cannot exist without your circulatory system, an organization's financial system cannot exist without its marketing system. Additionally, changes to one subsystem affect other subsystems.

This is the nature of any complex system, and organizations are complex systems. Each of the subsystems needs the others in order to function as a whole—the organization (see Figure 4.2). Therefore, by viewing the organization as

Systems and Subsystems

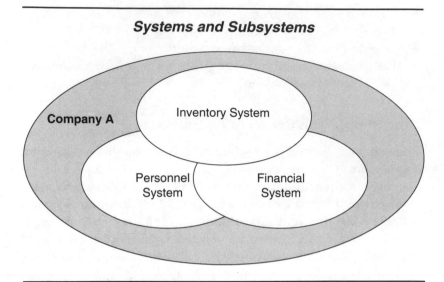

Figure 4.2 The standard definition of a system is any rational combination of parts or elements combined into a whole. Each system in an organization does not constitute the organization in and of itself. In other words, the financial system alone does not define the organization, nor does the personnel system alone. Even when analyzing portions of a system such as a specific process or department, an holistic view must be maintained.

a complex system made up of interrelated subsystems, arbitrarily making changes to one part (subsystem) of the organization will affect other parts (subsystems) of the organization. Business process redesign concepts as well as systems analysis techniques take this interrelatedness of the subsystems within an organization into account. Systems analysis techniques based on the SDLC (System Development Life Cycle) approach provide a framework for problem resolution on which business process redesign is based.

Whenever you are solving a problem, you must determine whether the solution will affect other areas in the organization. You don't want to redesign a process which will reduce the work load of one department while doubling it in another. A holistic viewpoint should be taken when redesigning processes. Even if the scope of the project is narrow, how the changes will affect other areas within the organization should be addressed. This is time-consuming but necessary. Management must be aware of what each department is doing. If the holistic viewpoint is not taken, each department may make changes and ultimately, more confusion could result because causes and effects have not been taken into consideration. Remember, each department and process is only a part of the whole organization.

Solve the Problem

No matter how well thought out the resolution to a problem is, if it is not implemented it is useless. Both follow-through and follow-up is critical in any problem-solving scenario. When resolving business problems, and ultimately redesigning how things are done, it is important to implement the changes as well as assess them. In other words, if processes have been redesigned and changes implemented, those changes should be reassessed—did the changes solve the initial problem? In many instances the initial problem still exists. One way to ascertain whether an actual problem was resolved or just a symptom of that problem is to determine if the problem still exists after the solution is implemented.

For example, one organization set out to solve its collections problem. The company analyzed the collections process and redesigned the system to be more efficient. New software and computer systems were installed and personnel were trained. The redesigned process was then assessed. When the accounts receivable aging report was examined, the number of delinquent accounts had actually risen! How could this be? They had followed through on the implementation, they included training in their plans, what else could they do?

The assessment step of any project will help you to determine whether the problem was actually addressed or only a symptom. In this case the actual problem was not a collections problem but a billing problem. If the problem is not correctly identified at the beginning of the project, enormous amounts of time and resources can be spent working on the wrong things!

SYSTEM DEVELOPMENT LIFE CYCLE APPROACH

The systems development life cycle concept (SDLC) is used in information systems development, whether structured analysis, information engineering, or object-oriented development techniques are used. The SDLC can be thought of as a problem-solving technique. It provides a framework for working through problems with an emphasis on information systems development (see Figure 4.3). However, the concepts involved can be applied not only to computer information systems, but also to the development of any new or redesigned systems in an organization, manual or automated.

Many companies and consulting firms that market a methodology address all phases of the systems development life cycle with step-by-step procedures, deliverables, and preferred tools and techniques identified. Deliverables denote a physical representation of the conceptual systems work accomplished to a certain point. Some examples of deliverables are feasibility reports, systems proposals, sign-off documents, and system design alternatives. Deliverables are documents or models used to represent the conceptual work of redesigning or creating a business process or system. It is a way to measure the progress of a systems development project and to determine whether deadlines will be met. Some form of deliverable is necessary in any project if it is to be managed effectively. Without some time frames and specific documents or models identified for completion, how can you judge whether a project is on schedule?

The SDLC can be divided into major phases. The tasks in these phases are divided and grouped differently depending upon the commercial methodology chosen. Some popular current methodologies are STRADIS, Method/1, CARA, and Navigator. However, for purposes of discussion, a generic SDLC will be overviewed. All methodologies which address the SDLC contain the following functions even though they may be labeled differently.

☑ *Planning*

☑ *Analysis*

Overview of SDLC (System Development Life Cycle)

System Development Life Cycle (SDLC) Phases	Issues Addressed by each Phase of the SDLC
Planning	Determine if proposed project supports the strategic goals of the organization and has the support of senior management.
Analysis	Determine the scope of the proposed project and what the processes under investigation should accomplish. Distinguish what the system should do rather than how it will be accomplished.
Design	Determine how the redesigned system or processes will be implemented. Identify if outside assistance for program development will be necessary as well as if any additional hardware or technologies will need to be acquired.
Implementation	Purchase any technologies, acquire any consulting services, and code any programs identified in the design phase. This phase gets the job done.
Maintenance/ Evaluation	Determine if the redesigned system was successful. Assess the value of the changes implemented and determine if further changes or modifications to the processes under consideration are necessary.

Figure 4.3 Business reengineering projects follow the SDLC. They are based on both the SDLC model and the traditional business problem-solving model. Understanding the concept of the SDLC helps to put into perspective the tasks and phases of a business reengineering project.

☑ *Design*

☑ *Implementation*

☑ *Maintenance/Evaluation*

Business process redesign projects also follow the same basic SDLC phases just outlined with some additional detail tasks or steps. Business process redesign (BPR) projects place greater emphasis on certain tasks in the SDLC, specifically, those which concentrate on what needs to be done and question why certain procedures are in place. Chapters 5 through 8 address the specific steps or tasks involved in a business process redesign project. The SDLC can be thought of as a plan to develop a system. Using the analogy of a builder, the SDLC in this case would be analogous to the guidelines and rules an architect would use to draw up blueprints for a building. The SDLC is not the actual system design, just as the plans to draw the blueprint are not the building specifications. The SDLC provides guidelines, provokes questions, and serves as a framework for problem-solving. Each of the phases can be mapped to a correlating step in business problem-solving (see Figure 4.4).

Planning

The planning phase is the starting point of the SDLC. This phase ties any project into the overall mission of the organization. The vision of the organization should be articulated in a mission statement. It is assumed that your organization has a clear direction of where it wants to be in the market and what its mission is. This overall organizational direction must be tied to any projects, especially redesign projects, in order for the organization to reach its goals. Developing a mission statement or vision for the organization is beyond the scope of this book. However, there are books devoted to the topic of writing mission statements and determining vision for an organization.

The planning phase allows for issues such as the following to be addressed.

♦ Is the proposed project in sync with the vision of the organization as articulated through the mission statement?
♦ Does the proposed project have the commitment of upper management?
♦ Does the proposed project relate to any existing systems development projects or redesign efforts currently underway?

Business Reengineering projects combine the best of both worlds!

System Development Life Cycle (SDLC) Phases	Business Process Redesign (BPR) Phases	Traditional Business Problem Solving
Planning	Planning Phase Strategic planning	Strategic Planning
Analysis Requirements Definition	Redesign Phase Requirements Definition	Problem Identification
Design Tactical Planning	Transition Phase Identify Alternatives Develop Action Plans	Identify Alternatives Develop Action Plans
Implementation	Implementation Phase Project Management	Project Management
Maintenance/Evaluation Assessment	Implementation Phase Continual Improvement	Continual Improvement

Figure 4.4 The phases of structured analysis which are based upon the system development life cycle (SDLC) can be mapped to business process redesign (BPR) steps which are based upon both traditional business problem-solving techniques as well as the SDLC. Business reengineering projects attempt to consolidate ideas from both information systems development and traditional business problem-solving.

♦ Does the proposed project have the potential to change or affect other functions or subsystems within the organization?

Planning is a vital component of any project, especially redesign projects. Without planning and central control of redesign projects, confusion and duplication of effort may increase. Just as you need to plan your day to be productive, you need to plan and coordinate various projects and efforts underway within your organization to ensure there is no duplication of effort. Additionally, if you have several redesign teams working simultaneously, you need to ensure that the processes they are reviewing do not involve the same departments and processes. Not only do you need to be aware of the possibility of redundancy of processes redesigned, but you may also be trying to hit a moving target. The holistic viewpoint is important, even though you may only be analyzing a portion of the organization.

If a process which affects another process is redesigned, both are changed. For example, if you are redesigning your inventory systems and your sales system simultaneously, coordination must be in place. If while redesigning your sales system you determine you will sell your product before it is produced, focusing on customizing your product, the inventory system will drastically change. Any redesign efforts based upon the assumption that the inventory system would need to contain several months worth of products would be useless because of the changes the sales system caused to the inventory system. Senior management or a central office should complete the task of coordinating projects in order to encompass the broadest view of the organization. Many redesign projects cross traditional departmental lines. Without seeing the big picture it is difficult to determine how everything fits together.

Analysis

The analysis phase of the SDLC identifies the starting point of a project once it is determined that the project meets the goals of the organization. In other words, projects are identified in the planning phase and the project itself begins in the analysis phase. The analysis phase is the portion of the SDLC that addresses what the problem is, what the scope of the project will be, and what the desired outcome of the new system will be. The specifics of how the system will be developed is determined in the next phase, the design phase, of the SDLC. Even though the SDLC is geared toward computer information system development, the concepts can be applied to any project which begins by meeting the corporate goals and follows through to becoming an integral part of the organization. Analysis allows for the following type of issues to be addressed.

♦   What problem will be resolved or what opportunity will be seized?
♦   What is the scope of this project? What departments, policies, procedures, and personnel are involved?
♦   What does the existing system do? Which portions are automated, and which are manual?
♦   What should the new system accomplish? Will the new system be manual, automated, or a combination of both?

Although the analysis phase of the SDLC is the phase that should take the longest, in actuality, this is the most often neglected phase. In computer information systems development, the impetus is to see something tangible, to start programming. Therefore, many times the analysis phase is shortened, and design and implementation are started sooner than they should be. However, the analysis phase, determining what the system needs to do still has to be accomplished. If it is skipped over, the analysis is completed during the time allocated for the programs to be written, the implementation phase (see Figure 4.5).

Understanding the actual problem or opportunity and determining the requirements of the redesigned system represent the most critical phase of the SDLC. During the analysis phase many organizations hire external consultants in order to provide an objective analysis of their existing systems and to help them determine for themselves what their newly designed systems should accomplish. During this phase some design is also done at a high level of abstraction. Details of how the system will be developed are determined only as generalizations, such as what type of computer platform will be used, are decided. Automated portions of the new redesigned system will be determined at this time. Also, enabling technologies which would allow procedural changes to take place would be investigated at this time. If the new system or redesigned process is not built upon a solid analysis foundation, it will be doomed for

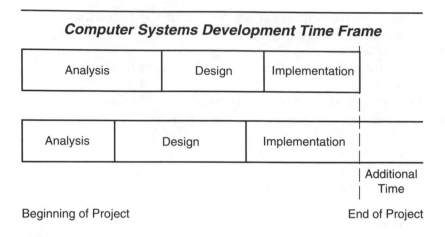

Figure 4.5 The total time frame of a computer systems development project is extended if the analysis phase is cut short. If you don't understand what needs to be accomplished, you will not be able to effectively design and implement a successful system. The same logic holds true for business process redesign projects. You must spend the time to fully understand the problem or opportunity under consideration before applying technology or redesigning processes.

failure. Just as the foundation of a building must be solid, the requirements of a system must be fully uncovered and understood in order to provide a solid foundation on which to build a new system or process.

Design

The design phase of the SDLC determines *how* the system or redesigned business process will be implemented. It completes the specifications for the new system or identifies how the essence of the system will be implemented. In traditional methodologies using the SDLC concept, the design phase includes writing programming specifications. Models are developed in the analysis phase and defined further during the design phase. Programming modules are identified with pseudo-code written for each module. **Pseudo-code** is an

English-like representation of programming logic used when a specific language has not been identified or when logic must be conveyed from a systems analyst to a programmer.

In more modern methodologies that follow information engineering techniques the emphasis in design is shifted from program logic to database design. However, program logic is still an integral part of the process, since it is still assumed an automated system is the answer. The emphasis continues to be placed on designing a computer information system because the SDLC is based on developing a computer information system. With the emphasis shifted from the computer programs within the system as the center of the process to the data and requirements of the system taking the focal point, the design phase can be altered to accommodate business process redesign projects. In other words, focusing on what the process should do and the data required to do it allows the emphasis to shift from writing computer programs to designing business processes, regardless of whether they are manual or automated.

Rather than only designing a computer system, manual procedures and policies, as well as partially automated subsystems, can be designed. Also, department structures and reporting structures may be changed within an organization to fully take advantage of the new redesigned business processes. Design can cover a great many areas; depending on the viewpoint taken when designing the system. Many systems will consist of a combination of redesigned business procedures, new automated systems, and shifts in personnel responsibilities. This phase addresses the following types of issues.

- How will changes such as new computer systems, changed procedures, and reassigned personnel functions be implemented?
- Does any portion of systems development or training functions need to be outsourced?
- Is outside assistance such as consulting services required to either determine requirements, design, or implement the system?

◆ Have any new problems in the analysis phase been uncovered?

During design, any requirements that were missed during the analysis phase should be uncovered. Plans for implementation also need to be developed. If major changes will
be introduced, how this impacts the employees must be considered and built into any training plans. How the new system will be introduced to employees is critical. One major
factor determining how the change will be introduced to
employees is the extent of the change. If minor changes will
be implemented, effort should be made to provide a transitional period for employees. Sometimes, if major changes in
employees' responsibilities and work environment will be
introduced, it is beneficial to introduce the change all at
once in order to minimize resistance to change. Finally,
training plans and implementation plans need to be developed during this phase to ensure an orderly transition.

Implementation

The implementation phase of the SDLC is the portion that
gets the job done. After it has been determined *what* should
be done (analysis phase), and *how* it will be done (design
phase), it needs to *be* done (implementation phase). The implementation phase addresses the following types of issues.

◆ Has the implementation plan been developed and accepted? Is the implementation plan on schedule?
◆ Have contracts for outsourcing services or equipment
been completed?

Ideally, this phase should not uncover any problems that
have not been addressed in the analysis and design phases.
The purpose of the SDLC is to provide a framework for
systematically developing systems. In projects adhering to
the traditional computer-based development views of the
SDLC, including information engineering, implementation
would cover installing hardware, writing and debugging pro-

grams, and creating databases. However, if the emphasis is shifted to a business process redesign project, technology may or may not be the focal point. In a business process redesign project a computer system may be a central part of the redesign, or the redesign may be totally manual such as changes in departmental functions, personnel assignments, and procedures. Existing technology may remain in place, but in many cases the technology also changes. It should be reiterated, however, that computer systems and technology in general should not be the focal point of a business process redesign effort.

Maintenance/Evaluation

Many methodologies and textbooks indicate the SDLC complete at the implementation phase. However, if it ends at implementation several questions go unanswered.

- Has training and documentation been successful in helping employees make the transition?
- Have the changes been effective?
- Is ongoing training necessary for new employees and to reinforce new procedures with existing employees?
- Have any other problems occurred since the new system has been put in place?

The maintenance/evaluation phase addresses issues of continuous improvement and evaluation. Any SDLC, or commercial methodology based on the SDLC, should be evaluated and customized to each organization as an ongoing process. This book provides a framework for business process redesign projects in Chapters 5 through 8; however, it is a generalized approach. Tasks still should be customized to the unique needs of each organization and each business process redesign project. Any methodology followed to redesign business processes or introduce change in general, should be reassessed itself. The outcome of the project is dependent upon the validity of the process used to produce the outcome—in this case, a redesigned business process.

SDLC in Summary

In summary, the SDLC provides a framework from which many commercial methodologies have been developed, such as STRADIS and Method/1. It is the basis used for computer information system development within most organizations, whether formal or informal. It can also be viewed as a type of problem-solving approach which can be correlated to business problem-solving models. The SDLC is also the foundation used to develop the overall structure of the guidelines for business process redesign projects outlined in Chapters 5 through 8.

WHICH APPROACH IS BEST?

Which approach should be used? Actually, a combination of both is optimum. The guidelines provided in this book (Chapters 5 through 8) are based on the system development life cycle (SDLC) approach with a great deal of the concepts in the business problem-solving approach incorporated in the planning and redesign phases. Whatever approach is used, some formal type of documentation and note taking must be part of the process. If you cannot recreate the steps you went through to solve a problem, from inception through redesign and finally implementation, how will you reproduce your success?

Similarities/Differences

The two problem-solving approaches discussed here, both the traditional business problem-solving approach and the SDLC approach, are based on three simple steps.

- ♦ Determine what you want to do. What is the problem?
- ♦ Determine how you will accomplish this. How can it be improved/redesigned?
- ♦ Do it!

Of course, each of these three steps are not as simple as they seem. Determining what the problem is can take an inordinate amount of time. Symptoms usually are apparent, but problems tend to hide from view. Both approaches to problem-solving attempt to emphasize the need to determine what you want to do before actually making any changes. However, the business problem-solving approach emphasizes more of the probing and questioning to determine if you really are solving the correct problem. The SDLC approach used by most information systems analysts assumes you have identified the correct problem. The two approaches actually compliment each other. It is not an either/or situation between the two approaches. As mentioned earlier, the guidelines presented in this book use both approaches.

Food for Thought

Just as TQM (Total Quality Management) means different things to different people, problem-solving holds different connotations for different individuals. If you ask about someone's strengths in a typical interview question, invariably one of the responses will be problem-solving skills. Most people feel confident that they can solve problems. And it is true that most individuals presented with a problem can resolve it. The tricky part is identifying the actual problem, not just a symptom! This is a skill that must be learned and is difficult to teach.

Remember back to either your elementary math class or your child's. When problems were given, it was relatively easy to work through the computations and derive the answer. However, when word problems were introduced, the level of difficulty increased. At that point you had to determine what the real problem was, not just solve a problem that was outlined for you. This is a difficult skill. Using both techniques and concepts from traditional problem-solving as well as the SDLC approach can help you sort through the symptoms to identify the actual problem.

CHAPTER HIGHLIGHTS

✎ Solve the problem not the symptom. Defining and redefining the problem until it is clearly understood by all parties involved provides the mechanism for uncovering the problems. Many times problems only become apparent through their symptoms. For example, if a rash appears on your skin and you try to solve the rash as though it were the problem you may not succeed. You can buy cream and salves to place on the rash, but it will not go away if the real problem is an allergic reaction to some food such as strawberries. In this case, the real problem is the allergic reaction; by simply treating the symptom (rash), the underlying problem is not addressed, and therefore not solved. The solution to this problem is not any type of topical treatment that can be placed on the rash, but rather a change in diet.

✎ It is not important to determine whether the issue you are addressing is a problem or opportunity. It is more important to differentiate between problems and symptoms. What may be viewed as a problem to one individual or organization may be deemed an opportunity to another. For instance, if one organization's sales are declining, it is a problem to that organization. However, for that organization's competitors it is an opportunity to increase their market share. It all depends on your perspective as to whether the issue you are addressing is a problem or opportunity.

✎ There are some prime times when business reengineering should be done. When an organization is downsizing or merging with another company, it is a good time to reassess processes and procedures.

✎ In order to solve a problem it must be succinctly defined. Identifying the scope of the project helps to determine the problem itself.

✎ The business problem-solving approach emphasizes problem definition and determining that the problem is not a symptom.

✎ The SDLC approach is primarily used in information systems development and emphasizes the cohesion of the various phases. In other words, analyzing what needs to be done must precede determining how it will be done.

- Not all problems should be solved using business reengineering. You must ensure that solving the problem will provide benefits to the organization and its mission.
- Even though analyzing a problem or redesigning a process focuses on a portion of the organization, a holistic viewpoint should be maintained. Each process or function within an organization affects another. This interdependency needs to be addressed when changing processes. Otherwise, changes in one portion of the company could adversely affect other portions.
- Follow through on changes. Assessing if the changes actually corrected the initial problem is vital. In many instances, you determine that you actually solved a symptom rather than a problem when you assess whether the redesign effort fixed the problem.
- The steps undertaken in a project based on the SDLC are planning, analysis, design, implementation, and evaluation. The steps outlined in this book for reengineering projects are based on the SDLC: planning, redesign, transition, and implementation. There is not an evaluation or maintenance phase in reengineering projects because the evolution is to a continual improvement model. After the process has been redesigned, it should be continually assessed and improved over time. Continual improvement should actually be built into the redesigned process rather than adding another step to the redesign project.
- The transition phase of the business reengineering model outlined in this book is based on portions of the analysis and design phases of the SDLC. The emphasis, however, is broader than traditional information systems development projects based on the SDLC. Business reengineering projects, even during the transition phase, focus not only on automated processes and data, but also on manual procedures, personnel, and policy issues.
- Both the traditional problem-solving approach and the SDLC approach to problem-solving are vital models. However, in order to leverage the best of both worlds, a

combination of the two, as outlined in Chapters 5 through 8, is preferred.

✎ Two of the most difficult parts of the entire business reengineering project are determining what project to focus on and ascertaining whether it is really a problem or a symptom of a larger problem.

PART II

Business Reengineering Guidelines

5

Planning Phase

Any project begins, or should begin, with a plan. Business reengineering is no exception. In fact, without a plan, nothing will be accomplished, confusion will result, and problems could actually be created rather than solved. Whenever you are dealing with the way people do their jobs, the culture in which they exist, and their sense of security, friction will result. Planning for these obstacles and contingencies is an important part of the project. Business reengineering projects contain four main phases (see Figure 5.1):

- Planning
- Redesign
- Transition
- Implementation

After implementation, continual improvement is incorporated into the redesigned process, so that this process does not become stagnant. You cannot continue to allocate the resources and efforts required to redesign the same process over and over again. Chapter 9 addresses the issue of continual improvement. This chapter focuses on the initial planning phase as well as addressing the need for ongoing tactical planning at the end of each phase.

Business Reengineering Guidelines Planning Phase

BPR Phases	Tasks within phases
Planning	Senior Management Commitment
	Determine Priorities
	♦ Organizational goals
	♦ Strategic plan
	Identify Scope
	Determine Initial Feasibility
	♦ Technical
	♦ Economical
	♦ Political
	Determine Potential Benefit
	Identify Core Team Members
Redesign	see Chapter 6
Transition	see Chapter 7
Implementation	see Chapter 8

Figure 5.1 These planning tasks provide a guideline for undertaking BPR (business process redesign) or business reengineering projects. However, this information must be customized by each organization in order to be effective.

ISSUES TO BE ADDRESSED

The planning phase is the first phase of the BPR model suggested in this book. Several planning issues must be addressed before a BPR project can begin. Obviously, the first step is to have a problem or opportunity for improvement identified. As mentioned in Chapter 4, downsizing or company mergers may be a unique opportunity to apply BPR concepts in order to create a more effective organization. There are many other opportunities or problems, however, which merit undertaking BPR concepts. As discussed in Chapter 4, the problem must be succinctly defined and determined to be an actual problem and not a symptom. Once that is done and you have an actual problem to resolve or an opportunity to take advantage of, the reengineering process begins.

Senior Management Commitment

In order to be successful, any BPR project should be initiated by senior management, who must determine which processes are potential candidates for undergoing redesign. As discussed earlier, not all problems are solved through reengineering efforts. Potential projects may be brought to senior management's attention through recommendations from middle management and staff. Sometimes, senior management may elect to have an objective, outside consultant provide a list of possible redesign projects. In any case, some idea of the types of processes or systems which the organization should contemplate redesigning must be identified.

Determining Priorities

Once senior management has a list of potential projects, the next task is to determine which ones will go through the redesign process and in which order. An effective way to make this decision is to match the proposed projects for redesign against the strategic plan or organizational goals of the institution. A matrix is a useful technique to help determine which proposed redesign projects correspond to the overall goals of the organization.

Of course, the matrix is only a tool to be used with your expertise and judgment. If you reduce the decision-making process to a numbers game, problems can arise. The matrix technique, if used, should be only one aspect of the decision-making process. Just as financial planners and analysts do not rely on one ratio or technique, neither should business decision-makers. Financial planners will use ratios, analyzing the profit and loss among other factors, but they will still use qualitative insight as well. Their expertise and "feel" for the market are part of the process of recommending stock

---

Goals by Project Matrix

| | Organizational Goals | | |
Potential BPR Project (function)	Increase Sales in International Market	Reduce Overhead	Improve Product Quality
Raw materials purchasing system	X	X	X
Customer ordering system	X		
Hiring and recruitment process		X	
Decentralization of sales offices	X	X	

Figure 5.2 The matrix is simply a table which compares two variables; in this case, the organization's goals and potential business reengineering projects. By using a tabular method to compare these two variables it is easier to determine which project should be evaluated first. In this case, the raw materials purchasing system should be the first project to be evaluated for feasibility based on the fact that it meets all three of the corporate goals. Matrices, as business reengineering techniques, are discussed further in Appendix A.

purchases. The numbers alone will not give them the entire picture. Neither will the outcome of a matrix analysis. You may decide to choose a project that does not meet most of the goals as identified by the matrix analysis; however, there are other circumstances to take into account as well.

For instance, the proposed raw materials purchasing system (see Figure 5.2) may not be the best choice at this time, even though it meets all three of the organizational goals. If the company is planning to develop a new product line, or major growth in the near future, maybe the hiring and recruitment process should take precedence. Analyzing the various projects by placing them in a matrix and matching organizational goals to projects should be a starting point for discussion. Other factors within the organization should also be considered when deciding which projects to undertake first. The scope of the project, as well as feasibility must be considered.

Once a potential project has been identified there are several aspects of the planning phase which must be addressed: scope, feasibility, benefits, and team assignments. It should also be noted that once a potential project is identified, it may never proceed any further than the planning phase. After a potential project is identified, the scope of the project is ascertained, and technical, economical, and political feasibility are assessed. At this point in the project, enough information may be gathered to either reject the project for redesign or to wait for a future time to address the project.

One institution was looking at all of its internal forms and the way in which these were routed within the organization. The scope of this project included all paper forms and some electronic forms that were used internally. Forms such as purchase requisitions, travel requests, and vacation requests were within the scope of the project. Rather than simply automating the existing forms, the project was focusing on eliminating, combining, and changing the forms themselves and eventually automating the redesigned forms. Since the number of signatures required on each form was also within the scope of the project, a way to eliminate some of these signatures, sometimes up to fifteen per form, was investigated.

The project progressed through planning and determining feasibility, at which time it was decided by senior management to wait until a later time to complete this redesign project. It was not that the project did not meet the goals of the institution; however, after the political feasibility was analyzed it was determined that the individuals who would need to be involved in this project were already involved in installing a newly purchased computer information system and evaluating their current office procedures in order to effectively utilize the new system. Senior management felt that there were too many projects which middle management and administrative staff were working on and they did not want to add additional pressures.

Whenever deciding which projects and processes to undertake as business reengineering projects, all aspects need to be addressed. Group discussions are a useful way to gather information; however, one-on-one discussions with senior management prior to any group discussions are also beneficial. In many cases, people are reluctant to state the actual reasons why they may not support a specific project targeted for redesign in a group meeting, but on a one-to-one basis they will more often than not provide an honest assessment of the situation. As mentioned earlier, deciding which projects should be targeted for redesign is a crucial issue. If you are unsure of which of a few projects should be targeted for redesign efforts, you may request a preliminary assessment of the scope and feasibility of each of the projects you are trying to decide between.

Scope

BPR projects can be defined by their scope, as discussed in Chapter 2. The scope of a project is critical in determining feasibility, benefit, and team assignments. It also helps to determine whether the project is solving a problem or only a symptom. Scope is a critical concept that must not only be understood, but also agreed upon by all participants in the BPR project.

The scope is determined by placing boundaries around what is included and, just as importantly, what is excluded from the project. An overview data flow diagram is an excellent model to help illustrate the scope of a project in order to gain consensus. Data flow and overview diagrams are discussed in Appendix A. (Many of the techniques discussed in this chapter through Chapter 8 are further explained in Appendix A.)

The scope of the project may change when further analysis is completed in the redesign phase of the BPR project. However, if the scope alters enough to change the type of project (technology application, work-flow analysis, BPR, reengineering), then reassessment must be made by senior management. In order for a project to be undertaken by an organization, a derived benefit must be assessed. If the scope of the project drastically changes, the benefit of the project will also be affected. If this should occur, senior management should be made aware as soon as possible so that they can determine whether to continue the project or disband it.

The scope of a project must be determined before further planning can be done. If the scope is limited and it is determined that the project is one of applying technology to an existing process, then you will not want to expend considerable senior management time on a project of such limited scope which will not yield major benefits. The project should be assigned to the IS department if the underlying business process is not being changed and automation is occurring. However, if a project crosses the boundaries of existing departments and the potential for benefit is great, the risk of expending valuable resources is reduced because of the anticipated payback. If the scope of a project is too small, it will not be important enough to merit the time and commitment necessary to complete a BPR project. BPR concepts could be applied to intra-departmental projects; however, cross-departmental teams would not be established.

Feasibility

Various types of feasibility must be determined before a project can move forward. The feasibility issue is initially addressed during the planning phase; however, it is again addressed in more detail during the redesign phase. Figure 5.3 identifies the various types of feasibility.

Technical Feasibility

Technical feasibility may or may not apply during the planning phase. Even if, initially, a project under consideration looks as though it cannot be implemented because of technology limitations, the project should not necessarily be disregarded. Many times, once a process is redesigned, tech-

Issues Addressed by Different Types of Feasibility

Type of Feasibility	Issues Addressed
Technical	Does the technology exist to implement these changes? Is it affordable?
Economic	Can the project be undertaken within certain time, money, and personnel constraints?
Political	Is senior management in agreement on investigating alternatives to this process? Are there any underlying issues such as conflicts between department management?

Figure 5.3 Feasibility is first addressed during the planning phase of the BPR project. However, it is continually assessed throughout the project as more detailed information is uncovered. All three types of feasibility should be ascertained in order to determine if the project should continue. Even if senior management initially approve a project, feasibility issues must be assessed. Many times, after investigating the feasibility of a potential reengineering project, it is not appropriate to continue. Costs may be too great, benefits may not be great enough, or the technology may either be too expensive or nonexistent at the time.

nical solutions that were previously unavailable, become viable. Therefore, at this point in the project, technical feasibility should be considered, but not necessarily be the deciding factor.

If internal staff do not have the knowledge of existing technologies and how they could possibly help redesign a specific business process, outside consultants may be required. Appendix B provides an overview of some of the existing technologies which are being applied at different organizations to help redesign their processes. Technical feasibility is an important aspect of the redesign process, because in most instances the redesigned process will incorporate some type of new technologies. However, as mentioned earlier, you must be aware of new technologies and how they may help redesign processes. The driving force should not be the technology. In some cases, technical feasibility may not even be an issue. Processes can be redesigned without applying any new technologies, but that is rare.

Economic Feasibility

Economic feasibility addresses the issue of whether it is cost-effective to proceed with the proposed project. Estimated time and expenses should be calculated at this phase of a BPR project. It should be understood that the estimates provided at this phase of the project will be just that—*estimates*. It is impossible to provide precise figures for the entire project when the scope of the project may change once further information is accumulated in the redesign phase. However, a rough estimate of time and cost should be attainable. The BPR project phases presented here do not flow in one direction, such as the "waterfall" methodologies of the past. It is an iterative process. Planning is continually revised throughout all phases. The flow of the BPR project phases is more analogous to a coil unfolding rather than to a set of sequential tasks.

Political Feasibility

Political feasibility is often overlooked, but it is critical to the success of any project, especially one that is championing change. Political feasibility addresses the issue of whether there are any underlying issues related to a certain system or process. If senior management is divided on whether certain processes should exist within an organization in their present form or at all, then these underlying political issues could hinder the success of the BPR project. For example, any proposed projects which include hidden agendas or disagreements between management should be avoided or addressed and settled first, at least as far as initial BPR projects go.

The first few projects undertaken must be chosen not only for the value the redesigned systems would present to the organization, but also for their ability to succeed. Successful BPR projects are the best internal advertisement for inducing individuals to embrace changes in their existing processes. Political feasibility also includes estimating the level of acceptance by management to a proposed change. How managers and staff feel about the problems or systems under discussion must be considered. Many times, processes which are ineffective are also hard to change because the change may eliminate the part of the job people most enjoy. If change means giving up something you enjoy doing or your staff enjoys, the change will be much more difficult to initiate.

Benefit

After the scope of a project is determined and general feasibility questions have been answered, what's next? The opportunity to reap benefits must be a result of undertaking the project. If no benefits are anticipated, why would anyone undertake the project? Since people are creatures of habit and resist change, no one wants to change for change's sake alone. The benefits promised by undertaking BPR projects are increased effectiveness or productivity with reduced costs. That is an enticing carrot to hold out in front of hungry corporations engulfed in global competition. However, before moving forward with any BPR project, the potential benefits for that particular project must be clearly defined and articulated. Increased effectiveness and reduced costs are noble goals; however, they are definitely not quantifiable. In order to make a sound business decision based on estimated costs versus estimated benefits, more quantifiable benefits must be determined.

Traditionally benefit has been determined by either using tangible financial measures such as return on investment (ROI), payback analysis, present value analysis, or intangible qualifiable measures such as increased customer satisfaction and improved competitive advantage. Tangible measures are easier to justify and discuss. They can be quantified, tabulated, and compared readily. Intangible benefits, such as increased customer satisfaction, are harder to measure and to determine. Therefore, it is recommended that some form of tangible benefits be identified during the planning phase in order to ascertain whether the redesign project should be done. It is also imperative to have a quantifiable goal from which to reassess whether the redesigned project actually accomplished the desired effect. If you undertake a BPR project with the only goal or benefit identified as increased customer satisfaction, how will you determine if the BPR project was a success? Even if customer satisfaction has increased, can you verify that it was due to the redesigned customer support process or could it be attributed to other factors? Defining a quantifiable, attainable goal or benefit during the planning phase is one of the critical issues that should not be overlooked.

TYPES OF PLANNING

Planning is not something that can be done at the beginning of the project, then forgotten. Planning actually occurs throughout the entire redesign process. There are two different types of planning that need to take place: initial strategic planning and ongoing tactical planning. Strategic planning is all of the work that goes into a project before it is officially declared a project. If this definition is used, a great deal of the business reengineering work is done before a project is even identified. A great deal of time is spent in determining which processes and functions within an organization should be redesigned in order to provide the greatest payback to the organization as a whole. Tactical planning is ongoing throughout the project and is more specific.

Initial Strategic Planning

At the beginning of any project strategic planning takes place. This is the point where senior management must approve a project. Agreement upon the scope of the project and anticipated outcomes are determined. Also, at this point, determination as to whether a proposed project is in alignment with corporate goals is assessed. Remember, a business reengineering project should not be initiated if it does not meet the goals of the organization. For example, in an educational institution, a goal may be to increase enrollment by 10 percent for the next year. If a reengineering project is proposed that would allow faculty more time for research, then this reengineering project may be rejected by senior management unless they can correlate the proposed project and the goals of the institution.

Strategic planning occurs before a specific process or project has been targeted for redesign. At this point in the project decisions are made regarding which processes should be redesigned and what resources should be allocated. Some of the issues addressed at the initial planning of the project include the following:

♦ What problems or opportunities should be evaluated for redesign? A list of several options will surface.
♦ The problem or opportunity identified needs to be correlated with a process or function within the organization.
♦ Of the processes identified for redesign, which ones will provide the most benefit. This step should narrow the number of possible projects to three to seven.
♦ Using a matrix along with other decision-making techniques identify which project will be undertaken first.
♦ Once an initial project is identified resources need to be allocated. Who will work on the project? What is the expected time frame? How much funding is available? Can outside consultants be used at different phases of the project? Project management tools and techniques can help you address these issues. Basically, the questions that need to be answered at this point are:
  ◊ What (project identified)
  ◊ Who (assign initial team members)
  ◊ Where (identify if entire organization or portion thereof will be affected)
  ◊ When (set expected time frame)
  ◊ Why (identify payback to organization)
  ◊ How (identify methodology or model for reengineering)

♦ Determine how to introduce the reengineering project to the staff. Even before the project starts, support and buy-in are helpful. Some organizations have initiated "town hall" type of meetings where senior management addresses special issues such as business reengineering projects being contemplated so that the staff is aware of the projects currently underway and feels part of the team. Not everyone will be involved with every reengineering project; however, letting people know what is happening within the organization provides a great deal of support and eliminates rumors and, hopefully, resistance.

Ongoing Tactical Planning

Tactical planning is distinguished from strategic planning in two ways:

♦ By the level of detail of the plans
♦ By the ongoing nature of this activity

Tactical planning deals with the tasks that need to be accomplished within each phase of the reengineering project in order for it to be successful. This is ongoing planning that occurs throughout the various phases of the business reengineering project. The tactical planning for the redesign phase actually occurs in the beginning of the redesign phase. The following outlines the times in the reengineering project when tactical planning occurs.

♦ Planning Phase
♦ Redesign Phase
  ◊ Tactical Planning for Redesign
  ◊ Tactical Planning for Transition Phase
♦ Transition Phase
  ◊ Tactical Planning for Implementation Phase
♦ Implementation Phase
  ◊ Tactical Planning for Continual Improvement

Planning at the End of Each Phase

As mentioned earlier, tactical planning occurs throughout the entire project. During strategic planning enough information is not known in order to accurately plan time and resources for the next phase. As the processes and functions under consideration are evaluated and more information is obtained, the ability to plan becomes easier. For instance, the scope is identified during the planning phase of the project; however, more information is uncovered and the scope of the project is more succinctly defined during the redesign phase. If the entire plan was developed for each phase of the project during the planning phase, adjustments would continually have to be made—creating more, not less, work for everyone concerned. That is why it is recommended that the planning phase address the strategic, global issues of the project, and tactical planning be left for the end of each phase.

The reason tactical planning is not done at the end of the planning phase for the redesign phase is the composition of the team at that point. The planning phase is generally completed by senior management. Their time commitment is limited and their ability to view the global impact of projects is crucial in strategic planning, but not in tactical planning.

♦   Strategic planning addresses what resources are needed, what commitments are necessary.
♦   Tactical planning addresses how the plans can be implemented—how can we redesign this particular process?

Updating Overall Project Plan

Tactical planning not only addresses what needs to be accomplished during the next phase of the project, but also updates the overall plan. During the initial strategic planning phase an overview plan is developed. The questions regarding resources, time frames, and funding are addressed. At the end of each phase the tactical planning task is to assess the tactical plan for the next phase against the overall plan. For example, if at the end of the redesign phase, tactical planning occurred and it was estimated that it will take six months rather than three months to complete the transition phase of the project, then this time estimate should be assessed against the original time frame developed during the initial strategic plan. This information should be shared with senior management as soon as possible. If the project time frame or resources needed have drastically changed during tactical planning, everyone involved in the project should be notified. There may have been confusion regarding the scope of the project, or the complexity of the project may have become apparent as more information is uncovered.

You should not be afraid to identify changes in the initial project plan. As more information is uncovered, the initial plan may not be valid. For instance, one manager assessed the need for additional resources at a certain level and because of this assessment thought that an employee could be hired to fill needs in two different areas within the department. However, after investigating further and determining specific tasks that needed to be accomplished, it became apparent that two people, with two different skill sets were necessary. Detailed information can change the initial plan; you should be prepared for this occurrence. Senior management should also be made aware that the time and resource estimates provided during the planning phase of the project are just estimates, not promises.

The overall plan may need to be adjusted as the project progresses. Also, senior management may decide at any point that the project should be canceled. The tactical planning tasks within each phase provide an opportunity for feedback to senior management. At each phase the decision as to whether to continue the project should be addressed. Sunk costs should not be considered. Following is an outline of the time frame for decision-making by senior management concerning whether to proceed with the project.

♦ Planning Phase
  ◊ Scope and feasibility estimated
  ◊ *Decision Point*

- ◆ Redesign Phase
  - ◇ Scope defined further
  - ◇ What needs to be changed, not how it will be accomplished, is established
  - ◇ Tactical planning—estimate of resources for next phase
  - ◇ *Decision Point*
- ◆ Transition Phase
  - ◇ How the changes will be accomplished is established
  - ◇ Tactical planning—exact costs for implementation identified
  - ◇ *Decision Point*
- ◆ Implementation
  - ◇ Once the project progresses to implementation, continual improvement should follow. A decision whether to continually assess the project is not necessary. Continual improvement should be built into the redesigned process in order to alleviate the chance of obsolescence.

The concept of decision points throughout the process in order to ensure that the project remains on task and within certain resource allocations is important. There are countless examples of projects which are millions of dollars over budget and years beyond the estimated completion date. If the initial scope of the project is maintained, this type of nightmare should not exist. However, you want to be sure that you are controlling the project, not the project controlling you. Business reengineering projects can take longer than initially estimated because you are not dealing with just computer systems or engineering systems; you are dealing with people. The people-management aspect of business reengineering projects is the most time-consuming. People need to be kept aware of changes that will affect their jobs or they will become apprehensive. Cooperation will be difficult to obtain and the time to accomplish specific tasks may extend beyond the estimated time frames. All of these factors need to be taken into consideration when planning a reengineering project. Reengineering projects need continual monitoring and control in order to stay on task. Initial planning is critical, but so is ongoing, tactical planning to keep the project moving ahead.

SELECTING TEAMS

Core team members cannot be determined until after the scope of a project has been ascertained. Before core team members can be named by senior management, the departments which are within the scope of the proposed project must be identified. After the departments are identified, individual members within those departments should be determined, as well as their roles in the BPR project. Whatever individuals are named to the BPR project, they should have the responsibility as well as the authority to act on behalf of their department. In other words, whatever decisions made by the BPR project team should be made at the BPR project meetings without members having to go back to their departments to obtain authorization from superiors. Individual members of the BPR project team should be empowered to make the necessary decisions to move the project forward.

At the end of the planning phase initial team members should be identified. These core team members should then identify additional team members for the redesign phase during tactical planning at the beginning of the redesign phase. During tactical planning, for each phase of the project the core team members should determine the team composition for the next phase. For example, at the end of the redesign phase, during tactical planning for the transition phase, the *core* team members should identify who should be on the transition team. This may mean adding additional team members and removing some current team members. It is easier to complete this task if the individuals you are discussing are not in the meeting.

In one institution the composition for a team was being assessed between the redesign phase and the transition phase. One team member who was currently on the team did not have the skills necessary for the transition team. It would be in the best interests of everyone involved not to waste his time attending meetings where he could not contribute on a recurring basis. However, that individual felt it was important that he stay on the team for political reasons; he was therefore reluctant to relinquish his status. Since he was present at the meeting, he was able to justify why he should remain on the team. The rest of the team members felt that if he wanted to be on the team that much they would let him remain.

However, every organization has limited resources, and business reengineering takes a great deal of time on the part of the reengineering team. The work this individual was hired to do was not being completed while he was working on the team during the transition phase, where his particular expertise was not needed. The idea of a fluctuating team allows you to leverage resources. However, leveraging resources when the resources are people complicates matters. It is a more complex problem to leverage human resources than to maximize equipment usage. Personnel issues are relevant and need to be taken into account when using the fluctuating team model. If someone is no longer needed on the team, diplomacy and tact should be used. It is always easier to ask someone to participate than to ask that person to leave.

The fluctuating team membership should be reiterated at the beginning of each phase of the project. One useful way to ensure that everyone agrees is to have a "kick off" meeting with the core team members at the beginning of the redesign phase. This meeting should be planned during the initial strategic planning phase. The kick off meeting could take several forms, one of which may be the town hall meeting model. The information shared at the kick off meeting should also be shared with new rotating team members. It should be stated when new members are asked to join the team that their participation is only for the specific phase of the project for which they are being recruited. If they are needed on future phases, they will be asked to participate at a later time. Many individuals will be relieved to know that the level of their commitment will be limited. It is much easier, however, to ensure that new team members are made aware of the fluctuating team model the project is using, as they are assigned to the project.

CHAPTER HIGHLIGHTS

✎ Planning is an integral part of a business reengineering project. Planning occurs not only before a project is even identified, but throughout the entire business reengineering process.

✎ The planning phase is the first phase of the business reengineering project. It is the phase of the project that identifies which processes will be redesigned and what resources will be allocated.

✎ In order for the planning, and the BPR (Business Process Redesign) project to be successful, senior management must be involved. Commitment from senior management is critical to the success of business reengineering efforts. The larger the scope of the project, the more necessary it becomes to have senior management's involvement and support.

♦ Business Reengineering (senior management support critical)

♦ Business Process Redesign (senior management support critical)

♦ Work-Flow Analysis (senior management support desirable)

♦ Technology Application (senior management support desirable)

✎ Potential projects need to be identified. A matrix is a useful technique to help you determine which potential projects support organizational goals. However, developing a matrix should not be the only technique used to analyze which projects to undertake. Qualitative as well as quantitative measures should be used.

✎ Determining the scope of the project is essential to continuing the business reengineering process. The scope determines the outcome of the feasibility and benefit analysis, and helps you assess the composition of the core team.

✎ Once a potential project is identified, the feasibility of that project should be assessed. There are three types of feasibility:

♦ Technical feasibility

Does technology exist that can be applied to this project? Even if the answer is initially negative, the project should not be stopped based on this. During the redesign phase changes may occur which will change the initial assessment.

♦ Economic feasibility

How much will this endeavor cost? At this point in the project, only rough estimates can be obtained. There is not enough detail to determine exact costs; however, a ball park figure should be attainable. This cost figure will be refined during tactical planning at the end of each phase of the business reengineering project.

♦ Political feasibility

Are there current organizational issues which would affect this project? This feasibility is the type most often overlooked. However, it is the one that most often stops a project.

✎ Even if a project is feasible, it must benefit the institution in order for the effort to be worthwhile. Benefits should be assessed and quantified in order to determine whether the project has met its objectives. Both tangible and intangible benefits should be identified.

✎ There are two types of planning that exist within the business reengineering project. Both are equally important, they just serve different functions.

♦ Strategic planning addresses global, overview types of issues such as identifying which processes should be redesigned and what resources should be allocated. Strategic planning answers the question "What should be done?", but not how it will be accomplished.

- ◆ Tactical planning addresses the details needed to re-design a specific process or processes. Tactical planning outlines how the project will be accomplished and who will be assigned to the project.
- ✎ Tactical planning occurs at the end of each phase except the planning phase. Tactical planning for the redesign phase is done at the beginning of the redesign phase rather than at the end of the strategic planning phase because of the team composition required during the planning phase. Senior management is mainly involved in the planning phase.
- ✎ During tactical planning the overall project plan is updated and feedback is provided to senior management. The overall project plan may need to be reassessed or adjusted. This feedback provides an opportunity for senior management to decide whether to proceed with the project.
- ✎ During strategic planning a core team should be assigned to the specific redesign project identified in the initial strategic planning phase. The core team members should have the ability to add and remove team members throughout the project. This strategy allows resources to be leveraged, outside consultants to be called in at key times, and internal staff to limit their time commitment.
- ✎ The strategy of fluctuating team members allows maximum use of resources; however, there are people issues that need to be addressed. People's concerns should not be overlooked, but addressed through discussions.

6

Redesign Phase

The redesign phase of a BPR project is the essence of the project (see Figure 6.1). Changes to the way things are done are initiated in this phase. If processes remain the same, the transition phase of the project can provide technical solutions, but major changes to the underlying processes will not occur. The redesign phase is the portion of the project where new ideas are generated. Therefore, it is important that individuals with an open mind and differing points of view serve on the redesign team. Without different viewpoints and perspectives the ability to creatively solve a particular problem or take advantage of a particular opportunity will be lost. If everyone agrees on the same action plan and no one questions the rationale of that plan, more than one viable solution will not be identified. As stated earlier, it is important that several viable solutions or action plans are identified for any given problem because it increases the probability that innovative problem-solving will occur.

TACTICAL PLANNING FOR REDESIGN PHASE

Identify Additional Team Members

Because objectivity is such an important aspect during this part of the project, it is critical that a team member with an

Business Reengineering Guidelines Redesign Phase	
BPR Phases	**Tasks within phases**
Planning	see Chapter 5
Redesign	Tactical Planning for Redesign Phase
	◆ Identify additional team members
	Determine Scope
	◆ Analyze problem or opportunity
	◆ Customer emphasis
	Evaluate Feasibility in More Detail
	◆ Technical feasibility
	◆ Economical feasibility
	◆ Political feasibility
	Requirements Definition
	◆ What current process/system does
	Redesign Process
	◆ What new process/system should do
	◆ Brainstorming
	Redesign Recommendation
	Tactical Planning for Transition Phase
	◆ Identify key transition team members
Transition	see Chapter 7
Implementation	see Chapter 8

Figure 6.1   The tasks outlined provide a guideline for a BPR project. However, this information must be customized by each organization in order to be effective.

unbiased opinion be appointed to the project during this phase. It may be beneficial to use outside consultants at this point. They can provide an impartial opinion of current processes, as well as suggest possible redesign ideas. Many times, outside consultants are engaged for the purpose of identifying alternative ideas, since they have worked with various companies in similar situations. However, you should not rely on outside consultants to provide all the redesign ideas. Internal staff members, familiar with existing processes and open to new ideas and ways of working, are the best source of innovation. The formality of the BPR project is intended to provide an environment and context in which innovative staff can nurture their ideas and creatively solve problems. If an outside consultant is not brought in, someone who will not be directly affected by the changes should be involved in the redesign phase in order to provide this objectivity. Systems analysts already possess this objectivity and may be useful in this role as long as they do not have a propensity toward recommending automated solutions. Remember, technology should not be the driving force of a BPR project.

Redesign Phase Plan

Identifying team members is an integral part of tactical planning. However, plans including time lines and resources need to be determined at this time for the redesign phase. Project management tools are vital aids during the ongoing, tactical planning required by the business reengineering methodology outlined in this book. The tactical planning task incorporated into each phase answers the questions— who, what, when, where, and why. Without a plan, how can you determine if your project is on track?

Planning, as discussed in the previous chapter, involves not only the strategic, initial planning involved in selecting the project, but also the ongoing, tactical planning at each phase. The tactical plan is also an excellent tool to ensure that not only the team members, but also departmental management and senior management understand the time lines and resources required to complete the particular phase of the project.

DETERMINE SCOPE

The scope, feasibility, and benefits of a project are determined during the planning phase (discussed in Chapter 5). However, once senior management makes a commitment to a specific BPR project, the issues of scope, feasibility, and benefit must be reconsidered in more detail. The following sequence of events occurs between the planning phase and the redesign phase.

♦ Senior management was involved in determining if a project should be investigated and assigned key members to the BPR team.
♦ After key members have been identified, they may name others to their BPR team.
♦ The initial team members need to assess their strengths, as well as the tasks that will be required of them.
♦ After this self-assessment, the team, as a group should determine if additional members are needed.

The purpose of letting the team identify additional members is twofold. First, the team members are best able to ascertain their own strengths and weaknesses and determine what abilities are required by additional team members. Second, and just as important, the act of selecting and agreeing upon additional team members provides the first team-building exercise.

Teamwork is an integral part of reengineering; providing opportunities for team members to understand team work and begin making decisions based on consensus is vital. The ability of the initial team members to agree upon new members provides the building blocks necessary to begin brainstorming activities and other breakthrough thinking techniques within this phase of the project. Once the whole team is formed, the issue of project scope must be reevaluated. Scope needs to be determined before feasibility or benefits are reassessed because it directly affects them.

♦ In essence, the scope of the project determines what the project is.
♦ By defining the scope, the problem definition is identified.

Therefore, if the scope of the project is viewed differently by the redesign team, then the feasibility and ultimately the benefits will also change. The scope may also appear different at this time because the team members may have more detail about the existing processes under consideration.

Analyze Problem or Opportunity

During the planning phase, senior management was involved in covering the high-level, or general, aspects of the project. Even though the problem was identified and a preliminary scope determined by senior management at that time, enough detail was not known to determine whether the problem was correctly identified and, subsequently, whether the scope was accurate. As progress through the various phases of the BPR project is made, you become more aware of the issues and better able to grasp the depth of the project. For instance, when you meet with a building contractor and discuss what type of house you would like built, the contractor can give you an estimate; however, he will inform you that, without more specific detail, all he can provide is *an estimate*. The same is true of redesigning business processes. Initially, problem identification, scope, feasibility, and benefits are identified without very much detail, during the planning phase. This is necessary in order to determine if the project should be investigated further.

However, once a project has been identified during the planning phase the same issues (problem identification, scope, feasibility, and benefit) need to be reassessed in more detail during the redesign phase. A project may progress to the redesign phase, but after further analysis it may not move forward to the transition and implementation phases. Just as you wouldn't want to build a particular house until you work out the details and have a better understanding of the costs involved, you may decide that once more detail is uncovered, the benefits of a particular project do not outweigh the costs.

Further, the problem identified during the planning phase of the project may change. Once further analysis is completed during the redesign phase, the scope of the project may change because the problem initially identified was a symptom rather than a problem. For example, during the planning phase one organization determined that the problem was one of billing: Too much paperwork and time was being consumed to bill customers. The scope of the project was determined to be the billing and accounts receivable departments. A team was formed and they entered the redesign phase. During the redesign phase more detailed probing revealed why billing was a problem, why it took so long, and why it involved so much paperwork. After discussing the matter, and continuously questioning why, it became apparent that the billing function was not the real problem—but the symptom. The true underlying problem was a collections problem. After this revelation, the scope of the project was changed and the team members reassigned. However, the shift from addressing a symptom to addressing a problem was a major breakthrough. This is the type of focal shift that will occur during the redesign process. After the issues of problem identification and scope have been reassessed, the project should be defined from the viewpoint of the customer.

Customer Emphasis

Determining the scope or focal point of a project cannot be accomplished without identifying the primary customer of the process or system. In other words, who is the benefactor of change. Ultimately, it should be the primary customer or consumer who purchases or uses your product; however, in the past, many information system projects were developed to make the internal workings of the company more efficient, even if it meant additional steps on the part of the consumer or primary customer.

For example, have you ever tried to return a product to a company that asked you to fill out several forms, and without your receipt, there would be no possible way they could reimburse you? Do you believe procedures like this would be implemented in order to serve the customer better? Of course not; they were developed in order to streamline the record keeping and administrative work involved in returning merchandise. Of course, any company would not intentionally develop procedures and processes which are annoying to the customer; however, it is a fact that in many instances this has happened. If the focus is too narrow and the primary customer is not kept in mind, processes that are efficient from a bureaucratic viewpoint but ineffective from a customer viewpoint will develop. For instance, using the billing example provided earlier, the scope of the project changed from billing to one of collections. However, for whom the system is redesigned will greatly affect the processes put in place. If the collections process is redesigned with the company's collection department in mind, then extra steps may be necessary for the consumer to complete or full payment in advance may be required. However, because of marketplace competition a system or process that does not take into account the needs of the customer will not survive. If customers are required to pay in advance or in full for their merchandise, they will probably go to competitors unless the product or service is so much superior or unavailable anywhere else. If, however, the process is redesigned in order to alleviate the collections problem internally, but still focuses primarily on the external customer, a more customer-friendly process will be developed.

Primary Customer Concept

The importance of identifying the primary customer of the process or system cannot be overemphasized. The primary customer is the group which the process will principally serve (see Figure 1.2). The primary customer may be internal, such as executives who may be the primary customer for an ad hoc decision-making system or external, such as consumers who may be the primary customer for a rental car return process. *The primary customer should be the driving force behind the redesign.* For instance, if the rental car return process was redesigned to focus on internal procedures and lessen paperwork for staff without focusing on the primary customer—the consumer—the effort expended would not provide an effective redesigned process. The redesigned process may be efficient from the viewpoint of staff;

however, from the consumer's (primary customer) viewpoint, the redesigned process may still prove inefficient and time-consuming.

One way to determine the primary customer is to have facilitated focus group sessions with team members and other individuals involved with the project to decide upon *one* primary customer. Issues to keep in mind when identifying the primary customer include:

♦ The primary customer is not always the external customer. Some processes are totally isolated from the consumer. In these instances, the primary customer is more difficult to agree upon.

♦ What may seem apparent to one individual as the primary customer may seem ludicrous to another. It is therefore recommended that the BPR project team, as a group, determine the primary customer for the process they are redesigning.

♦ If you are trying to solve a business problem, it must be solved in a manner which provides benefit to the primary customer. In other words, if an internal business problem is solved by changing procedures, but those changes adversely affect the primary customer, the overall benefit to the organization will either be nonproductive or detrimental. Savings in one area becomes costs or lost revenue in another.

After the primary customer and scope have been identified, it should be determined if the project is still feasible.

FEASIBILITY

The feasibility of a project will change if the scope or problem identified changes. To use the analogy of a builder once again, if you contract for a three-bedroom ranch, then change the scope of the project to include an additional two bedrooms and a second story, you could not expect the builder to use the same cost structure. If you drastically change the scope of a BPR project, you must reassess the initial determination of project feasibility. The project has changed, and the issue of whether it is cost-effective, technically possibly, or politically acceptable needs to be addressed again. In the previous billing example, when the scope of the project contained the billing and accounts receivable functions, the feasibilities associated with the project were based on billing and accounts receivable. However, when the scope of the project changed and the focal point became collections rather than billing, the feasibilities needed to be reassessed.

Once a shift in scope is identified it may still be economically and technically feasible to continue with the project; it may not be politically feasible. In this particular example there was some resistance from senior management to emphasize the collections portion of the project. Political feasibility, or the ability of senior management to support certain directions, is critical to the success of any BPR project. Political feasibility is the one that most often changes if the focal point of the project shifts during the redesign phase.

REQUIREMENTS DEFINITION

The **requirements definition** is a term used in information system development. The concept behind this term is readily transferable to BPR projects. This is the portion of the project which determines *what* the system should do—what requirements need to be incorporated into the redesigned process or system? What is currently being done is examined in order to determine what the redesigned system must do.

In traditional systems development methodologies, this is the point in the project when *analysis paralysis* sets in. In other words, analyzing what and how things are currently done takes up the majority of the project time. *Analysis paralysis* denotes the continual task of over-analyzing what is being done or what needs to be done, but never moving forward to actually do anything. In order to avoid this phenomenon, a succinct tactical plan as well as a general strategic plan should be in place. Time lines and milestones can keep a project on task and avoid the temptation to over-analyze the situation.

Understanding the Current Process

It is important to study the current process to be redesigned in order to determine what the redesigned process will be required to do or change. However, you do not need to know, at a detailed level, how the current process or system works in order to redesign it. For example, if the identified BPR project was to redesign the current budgeting system, you would need to know what functions the current budget process included, such as a mainframe program, paper documents transmitted between offices, and spreadsheet applications used by various departments. This information is important in order to determine what functionality the existing systems and business processes provided to the various departments. However, it is not necessary to have a detailed understanding of how each component of the existing system works. In fact, it is beneficial if you do not know the details. In this example, you don't want to know how the mainframe application is programmed for the budget process.

♦ You should view existing applications, especially legacy systems, from a black box approach and analyze the information input to the program and output from it.
♦ Studying the logic of a legacy program would prove futile. Business processes have changed since the program was written.
♦ The program was written in order to effectively use computing resources of the time. Factors affecting why the program was written with specific logic probably have changed.
♦ You don't want to replicate the current system.

Study the existing systems and processes only to the level of detail that will allow determination of *what* the current process does, not necessarily *how* it is done.

As was mentioned earlier, systems or business processes do not exist in a void; they are affected by other systems, both internal and external to the organization. Examples of internal systems include payroll systems, ordering systems, and billing systems. Examples of external systems include governmental reporting systems and internal revenue systems. It is necessary to understand the information flowing from both internal and external systems to the BPR process under consideration, as well as the information flowing from the BPR process to other systems and processes. Since processes and systems are interrelated, it is important to understand the relationship between those processes both within the scope of the BPR project and outside the scope. In this way, the requirements of what any redesigned process must address can be identified. Figure 6.2 illustrates how

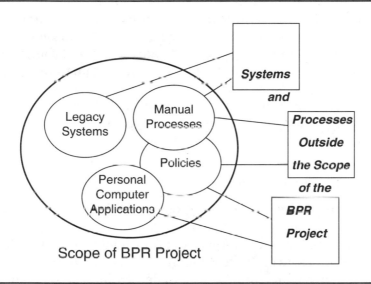

Figure 6.2 The processes within the scope of the BPR project must be understood at a conceptual level in order to determine what issues the new process must address. This diagram illustrates some functions that may be within the scope of a BPR project (legacy systems, manual processes, personal computer applications, and policies). It is not necessary to understand how the current processes and systems function, but it is necessary to understand what they do. The links between the systems within the scope of the project and those outside the scope of the project are also important. By analyzing the current processes and their links to processes outside the scope of the project, the requirements for the redesigned process can be identified.

the scope of the project determines the type of analysis that needs to be accomplished—legacy systems, manual processes, policies, and personal computer applications.

Maintaining Focus

At this point of the BPR project, it becomes necessary to stay focused on projected deadlines. While examination of current procedures is necessary, there is danger in becoming engrossed in capturing all the details of how a process is currently done within the organization and losing sight of the real goal—*changing* the way things are done. Thus, it is important to set time frames for how long you will spend analyzing current processes. Be sure not to look into too much detail when analyzing these processes. Understand what is being done without capturing all the details of how it is being done. For example, do not analyze current computer program logic or study each step a clerical person takes while filling out a form. This attention to minute details may or may not be required in later phases of the BPR project; however, you need to be sure to stay at a higher level of abstraction and focus on what is being done.

Applying Techniques

Some of the techniques that are useful during these tasks of the redesign phase include data flow diagramming, data modeling, and matrices. Appendix A provides more detailed information regarding these techniques. Data flow diagramming is a useful technique to help determine the scope of a project. However, detailed data flow diagrams should not be prepared at this time; only a high-level or overview diagram with just enough detail to help the team members understand what is going on is necessary. It is the task of the transition phase team to understand in enough detail how to implement the redesigned process. Data flow diagramming helps show the processes involved in the BPR project; however, it does not address the data required by the BPR process. It is therefore necessary to model the data as well as the processes. Data modeling techniques such as entity-relationship diagrams are a useful tool.

The benefit of using data flow diagrams (DFD) and entity-relationship diagrams (ERD), discussed previously, is that the information captured within these models can be directly used by information systems professionals, should some portion of the redesigned BPR process need to be automated. Many BPR projects utilize existing and emerging technologies to enable redesign changes. It is necessary, however, not only to understand the requirements of the BPR process under consideration, but also to be able to document that understanding in some meaningful way so knowledge can be shared between team members and individuals outside the BPR team. However, it is not a requirement to use these modeling techniques in the redesign phase.

Mandatory versus Desirable

Once requirements have been identified the following steps will help you determine which requirements are truly requirements and which are features which are desirable but not required.

♦ A list of all potential requirements from the existing system or process should be documented. One method to determine what the current process requirements are is to ask the question: "What does the current system or process provide that is still needed?"
♦ Once the list of current process requirements is obtained, then brainstorming to determine what the redesigned system should also provide should be conducted. Questions such as "What should the redesigned system or process do?" and "What would you like to see the redesigned process do?" should be asked.
♦ After requirements are determined, the identified requirements should be categorized. Certain requirements are mandatory, no matter how the processes will be re-

designed, while other requirements may be optional or desirable. A matrix could be created to determine which requirements are mandatory and which are optional.

The goal of the redesign phase is to look at creative ways to change *the way things are done* while maintaining the necessary inputs and outputs to the process. The goal of the transition phase is to determine *how* to implement the redesigned process. The matrix developed at this point is a useful tool during the transition phase. It helps determine which, of several, alternative implementation solutions is the best. Information gathered during each phase of a BPR project should be passed on to subsequent phases.

REDESIGN THE PROCESS

The redesign process is the heart of the entire BPR project. It is at this stage when breakthrough thinking, discussed in previous chapters, occurs. The redesign process is an additional step not incorporated into traditional information systems development methodologies. Some of the characteristics of this task include the following:

♦ Continuous questioning of why something is done a certain way.
♦ The BPR team needs to explore creative alternatives of what needs to be done so that new initiatives can be implemented.
♦ Remember, the goal is not to automate existing processes or to apply technology to existing processes, unless of course the scope of the BPR project is so narrow as to imply a technology application project instead of a BPR project.

As discussed in Chapter 5, the scope of the project defines the type of project it is. Figure 6.3 illustrates how a BPR project is defined by its scope. Depending on the type of project, the redesign tasks will differ greatly. When redesigning processes within the scope of a technology application project, there is little room for major change to occur. Policies and many procedures are outside the scope of the

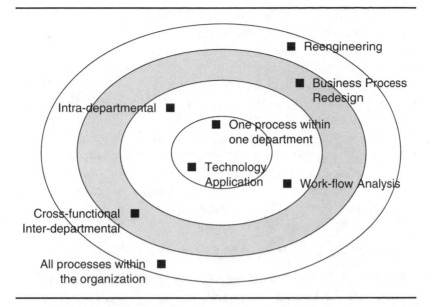

Figure 6.3 The scope of a project ranges from narrow to all-encompassing. Technology application projects have the narrowest scope as compared to reengineering projects which span the entire organization or a major portion of it. The scope of a project increases as more processes, people, and information are included in the project. The scope of the project directly affects what type of change can be introduced. The larger the scope, the more radical the change potentially could be.

project. However, as the scope of the project becomes larger, taking in more processes and procedures, the opportunity for making effective changes increases.

Computer Systems

There are several components and issues that need to be taken into account when redesigning business processes. There may be computer systems which have become integrated into the manual procedures of an organization. This is true for many organizations that have legacy systems. If computer systems were developed 10, 20, or more years ago, the functionality of the systems were limited to the technology of the time and the requirements of the organization. Of course, the organization has changed, and so has technology. Addressing these systems is an integral part of the redesign phase. The programming logic used to develop the legacy systems should not be analyzed. The system should be viewed as a black box and information input into and coming out of the system should be noted. The data files of the legacy system should be analyzed to determine what type of information is being captured and generated from the applications. It would be helpful to have someone with technical expertise on the redesign team if legacy systems are within the scope of the project.

Organizational Structure

Another component of a redesign project is the organizational structure. If the scope of the project is large enough to include several departments, the functions those departments perform should be reviewed, because organizational structures may change. A matrix depicting functions or processes within the scope of the BPR project and the departments responsible for those functions should be developed. When processes are redesigned, departments may be restructured or reporting lines altered. If the organizational structure is within the scope of the BPR project, it is helpful to have a human resources specialist on the team to address personnel policies related to restructuring departments. It is also imperative that senior management be kept informed.

There are many aspects to the redesign phase: Computer systems, manual processes, and organizational structure, have the potential for redesign. The redesign process itself can be accomplished in various ways. Some ways in which redesign initiatives can be fostered include the following:

♦   Bench mark external sources to determine alternative methods for accomplishing goals. Provide the team with ideas of how the processes could be redesigned. Even though the redesign team is not concerned with how to implement the changes, it is helpful for the team members to have some ideas of how other organizations have redesigned a particular process.

♦ Conduct brainstorming sessions to elicit innovative solutions to problems or opportunities. Various techniques for generating new ideas such as brainstorming, probing, and double reversal should be incorporated into the BPR project at this time.

♦ Bring in outside consultants to provide a fresh view of the problems and opportunities facing the organization.

The redesign task needs to become a natural follow-up to requirements determination of any proposed system or project. Once the requirements are determined, questioning should begin as to whether a particular problem should even be solved or the process eliminated. Look at the requirements before questioning process existence because mandatory information that needs to be given to another subsystem within the organization may be missed. Since no system exists alone, the possibility of changes in one system affecting another need to be continually investigated. If, after determining requirements, a design solution is developed, the opportunity to radically alter the way things are done is missed. Of course, following the steps outlined here does not guarantee that major changes will occur; however, the likelihood is increased. Once the scope of the project and the reason for the process itself are questioned and fully understood by the team members, it is time to determine what the redesigned system should do.

Brainstorming

How the change will be implemented should not be determined at this point. The emphasis is placed on *what* should be accomplished by the process under consideration for redesign (see Figure 6.4). Whether the redesigned solution should be outsourced, or a custom program should be written, or some other alternative should be chosen, is not designated at this time. *What* the redesigned process will accomplish is more important at this time. For this reason it may be helpful to

Redesign Phase	Transition Phase
Focuses on *what* needs to be done.	Focuses on *how* to do it.
Brainstorming and creative thinking are skills required during this phase.	Technical aptitude and attention to detail are skills required during this phase.
Outcome of phase is the redesign recommendation.	The redesign recommendation used as the starting point.

Figure 6.4   Differences between redesign and transition phases.

have a technology consultant meet with the redesign team during their brainstorming sessions in order to provide examples of how technology could be applied to various situations. For example, if you are brainstorming various ways to provide information to students on a college campus you may think of newspapers, electronic bulletin boards, or other types of information-delivery techniques. However, if someone knowledgeable about technologies were at the brainstorming session, that person may be able to interject such ideas as touch screen kiosks providing on-line student information, telephone registration, or student debit cards which provide automatic financial aid to be deposited into the student's bank accounts. Sometimes hearing ideas of what technology can do will spark ideas on how to change existing processes (see Figure 6.5). The next phase, the transition phase, addresses alternatives of how the proposed changes or redesigned processes will be implemented.

RECOMMENDATION OF REDESIGN

The recommendation which is a deliverable generated from the redesign phase is produced once the team determines what the scope of the new system will be and what the new

Figure 6.5 The redesign phase of a BPR project consists of determining what needs to be done without necessarily understanding how it will be accomplished. However, in some Instances it is difficult to imagine how things could be done differently because of a lack of understanding of existing technology and how it could be applied. Sometimes it is helpful to have a technology consultant meet with the redesign team during brainstorming.

system will accomplish. It is the point of the project when all the brainstorming ideas are assessed and consolidated into a single recommendation from the team.

The preceding redesign tasks allowed innovative ideas and alternatives to be investigated. Now those ideas need to be combined, eliminated, or fine-tuned into a single recommendation of what the redesigned process should accomplish. The outcome of this phase, the recommendation, is the starting point for the next phase, the transition phase. Once the redesign team identifies what the new process should accomplish, the transition team determines how the change can be accomplished.

TACTICAL PLANNING FOR TRANSITION PHASE

Tactical planning, as stated earlier, is ongoing and occurs at the end of every phase. The redesign phase is unique because tactical planning occurs both at the beginning and at the end of the phase. At the beginning of the redesign phase tactical planning is accomplished for the redesign phase itself. At the end of the redesign phase, tactical planning is accomplished for the next phase, the transition phase. The recommendation and the tactical plan for the next phase provide documentation for senior management to make a decision whether to proceed with the project. The tactical planning should include the following information.

♦ Determine a time line for the next phase. Since more detailed information is available after completing the redesign phase, a more precise time line and project management plan for the next phase can be developed.

♦ Determine resources needed for the next phase. Resources may include funds for training, consulting fees, hardware or software, and personnel.

♦ Adjust the overall project plan developed in the planning phase of the project to reflect any changes in estimated completion time or resources necessary.

♦ Identify team members for the next phase. The fluctuating team membership model should be used.

Fluctuating Team Membership Model

As discussed earlier, the outcome of this phase should not determine how the new system will be implemented. The composition of the team at the redesign stage does not include technical people unless legacy systems are involved; it usually does include the management and staff of the areas under discussion. Technical expertise is generally obtained during the redesign phase by inviting those individuals with the requisite knowledge to attend meetings or review documents and submit ideas. Technical experts may act as advisors, rather than team members, in the redesign phase. For this reason, the composition of the team does not contain the expertise to *apply* technologies to the desired outcomes. One of the benefits of dividing a project in this way is that scarce technical resource people can serve on multiple redesign teams, since they only need to be involved with the project for a short time. In most information systems development projects the systems analysts are involved throughout the project, which limits the number of projects they can work on simultaneously. By altering the team composition throughout the project, you can better utilize you technical personnel. The same logic can be applied to your business managers and various departmental staff members. Management's primary commitment is during the redesign phase; however, they will still be involved to a lesser extent during the transition phase of the project.

Identify Team Members

Team members will most likely change during the transition phase of the BPR project because the project's focus changes. The idea of teams changing as special needs are required is not new. In the medical profession, the operating room team is configured in this way. Specialists are called in during the operation when needed; however, certain individuals, such as nurses, provide continuity and are present during the entire operation. During the redesign phase management and staff familiar with the specific business areas being investigated are needed because the emphasis was placed on changing procedures, policies, organizational structure, personnel—in short, changing the way business is currently being operated. During the transition phase, the emphasis shifts to identifying ways to accomplish the changes recommended; therefore, staff with a knowledge of technology as well as procedural and personnel issues is imperative. By separating the redesign phase from the transition phase more flexibility in staffing the BPR project is allowed. If outside technological expertise is needed, you can limit the consultant's involvement and ultimately your costs.

Other personnel-related benefits occur when the BPR

project is divided by phases and team members can vary. Internal personnel with specialized technical or facilitation expertise can work on several BPR projects simultaneously, since their involvement is only required during a portion of the project. Figure 6.6 provides examples of the types of personnel which may participate in each of the phases of a BPR project, as well as the expertise required during each phase. Even if certain individuals are involved in different phases of the project, the nature of their participation will change. For example, senior management's involvement in the planning phase would vary from their involvement in the implementation phase. During the planning phase they would be involved with issues such as how a proposed project affects the strategic plans of the organization or how a certain project could assist with obtaining the immediate goals identified as critical by the organization. Their involvement during the implementation phase would mainly be concerned with facilitating change and providing support and funding for retraining, and other concerns that may arise during implementation. During the planning phase, senior management would staff the project and assign a project leader. Which individuals remain on the team after the redesign phase is completed may not be determined until the outcome of the redesign phase has been ascertained. Therefore, one of the first tasks to be completed in the transition phase is identification of team members.

The selection of previous team members should be reviewed to determine if they should be assigned to the transition team or if new members with new competencies should be named. Additions and deletions to the team membership list should be made appropriately. If a previous list of transition team phase members has not been developed during either the planning or redesign phases, it should be completed at this time. It is important that the team members reflect the direction the redesign process is taking. If the redesigned process is one that will rely heavily upon technology, several members who are versed in technology issues should be named to the team. If the scope of the project changes, or the main direction of the project is altered, then

Fluctuating Team Membership Model

BPR Phase	Possible Personnel Participating in the Phase	Expertise Required
Planning	Senior Management, Departmental Management, Technology Consultants, Business Process Redesign Consultants	Vision for organization, strategic planning, understanding of current technologies and applications
Redesign	Departmental Management, Departmental Staff, Business Analysts, Business Consultants	Open-minded, knowledgeable about the business and processes under consideration; able to look at problems and issues from a different perspective
Transition	Technology Consultants, Systems Analysts, Business Analysts	Logical thinking, ability to conceptualize models and designs, understanding of technologies and their applications
Implementation	Senior Management, Departmental Management, Systems Analysts, Programmers, Trainers, Technical Support Personnel, Human Resources Personnel	Detail-oriented, understanding of change and how it affects personnel

Figure 6.6 The composition of the team will change as the different phases of the BPR project are accomplished. Different expertise and skills are required during different times of a BPR project. By changing the composition of the team during the various phases, you can utilize your personnel more effectively. You can also limit the amount of time you may require an external consultant's expertise. It is a good idea, however, to maintain the same project leader throughout all of the phases of the project. There may also be a few core people that remain on the project for all or a majority of the phases.

it is only reasonable that team members should change. After the transition team has been identified, their first task is to identify alternative solutions.

CHAPTER HIGHLIGHTS

✎ The redesign phase of the business reengineering project is the core of the project. This phase allows major changes to occur which can provide the elusive goal of increasing profits and reducing costs.

✎ Diversity is the key to a successful redesign team. Differing points of view allow creative solutions to arise. Without constructive conflict, new ideas are not born.

✎ Tactical planning is completed at the end of every phase, except the planning phase because the planning phase is completed primarily by senior management. Senior management will identify a core team and that core team will provide tactical planning for the redesign phase, including selecting additional team members.

✎ During the redesign phase, additional team members who can provide objectivity should be chosen. Outside consultants and internal systems analysts can provide this type of objectivity. When changing the way things are done, individuals can become possessive and reluctant to change. It is beneficial to have a team member who does not have any stake in the outcome of the changes. For this reason outside consultants or internal systems analysts not directly involved with the departments being analyzed are good choices.

✎ Tactical planning includes identifying team members as well as other resources and establishing a time line for the phase. Tactical planning also includes updating the overall project plan. However, this is not a critical part of tactical planning during the redesign phase, since the project has not progressed far enough through the phases to warrant changes to the overall project plan.

✎ The core team members are selected by senior management during the planning phase. However, the core team members should be able to add additional members for the specific phase. Allowing the team members autonomy to select additional members helps build teamwork and strengthen the team.

- The team members themselves are best able to ascertain their strengths and weaknesses and thereby determine if additional team members are necessary.

- The scope of the project directly affects the feasibility and ultimately the benefits of the project. All of the team members, as well as management must agree on what the scope of the project is in order to move forward. Without agreement, management could have a totally different project in mind than the redesign team has in mind. There is a great deal of difference between a project that automates forms and one that revamps the entire authorization process and routing sequence of forms.

- The problem was initially identified and the issue of scope was addressed by senior management during the planning phase. However, an in-depth understanding of the problem was not completed at that time. Further investigation into the actual problem and scope of the project needs to occur during the redesign phase.

- The project may not progress to the transition phase after further analysis is accomplished. The actual problem and scope of the project may change after further investigation into the project itself is completed during the redesign phase.

- The primary customer should be the driving force behind the redesign process.

- Any redesigned process should not place additional burden on the primary customer. The primary customer can be internal or external to the organization.

- Identifying the primary customer provides focus for the team as they contemplate various redesigned processes.

- In order to avoid analysis paralysis, sound strategic and tactical planning should be in place. Knowing where you want to go and when you want to get there provides incentive for keeping on task and avoiding over-analyzing the situation.

- The current process or system should only be studied in

order to determine what it is doing in order to help define the requirements of the redesigned process or new system. Understanding the intricate details of how the current system works is not necessary at this time.

✎ Various techniques identified and described in Appendix A such as DFD and ERD cannot only help the redesign team understand existing and proposed redesigned processes, but also document it in order to communicate with others. Since redesigning processes is not a tangible process, having some type of tangible documentation to represent it is necessary.

✎ Requirements, or features of the new process should be identified and categorized. There are some features that are mandatory and true requirements. There are, however, some features that are desirable but not required, and this should be noted. When comparing different redesign options, it is important to note which features, such as reporting data to a federal agency, are required and which are desirable. Desirable features, such as electronic data interchange (EDI) capability should be noted; however, the entire redesign process should not be based on a feature that is not required.

✎ Part of the redesign process includes analyzing existing manual processes and computer systems as well as the current organizational structure.

✎ The redesign process can be achieved in several ways:
>   **Benchmarking**
>   **Brainstorming**
>   **Bringing in Consultants**

✎ Tactical planning for the next phase, the transition phase, is accomplished at the end of the redesign phase. Tactical planning includes:

◇   Identifying team members for next phase
◇   Determining time line for next phase
◇   Determining resources needed for next phase
◇   Adjusting overall project plan developed in planning phase of project

✎ The fluctuating team member model is used throughout the business reengineering project. A core team will provide consistency throughout the entire project. However, additional team members will join and leave the project depending on their expertise and the tasks required during the various phases. This fluctuating team member model provides the ability to leverage internal expertise as well as outside consultant's expertise.

7

Transition Phase

The transition phase begins after the redesign phase has been completed. During the transition phase members of the team may change. Emphasis is placed on planning *how* to implement the desired changes conceptualized in the redesign phase. In this phase traditional information systems development takes place. This is the phase of the business reengineering project where computer systems development takes place. Structured analysis techniques assume that the organization has thoroughly investigated alternatives before deciding if computer information systems should be developed. However, many times the redesign phase is skipped. Companies automate existing manual processes or update current automated processes without addressing the underlying business reasons—why the process is necessary in the first place. Remember, computerization is not an end in itself, but only a possible means of accomplishing reengineering.

In traditional computer systems development, manual processes and procedures are not questioned prior to bringing in systems analysts and programmers to develop automated systems based on what is currently being done in the organization. Without changing the processes, automation cannot provide any major breakthrough for the organiza-

Business Reengineering Guidelines Transition Phase	
BPR Phases	**Tasks within phases**
Planning	see Chapter 5
Redesign	see Chapter 6
Transition	Determine Alternatives
	♦ Strategic analysis
	♦ Strategic design
	Evaluate Alternatives
	♦ Evaluate solutions against requirements
	Tactical Study
	♦ Solutions proposal
	Tactical Planning for Implementation Phase
Implementation	see Chapter 8

Figure 7.1 The tasks outlined provide a guideline for a BPR project. However, this information must be customized by each organization in order to be effective.

tion. Certainly information can be processed quicker using computers, and information can be transmitted across the globe within seconds using telecommunications technology; however, a more important question would be to ask if the right information is being sent at the right time? The transition phase begins with the presumption that redesign questions such as these have been addressed. In a BPR project *what* needs to be done has been determined in the redesign phase; now, *how* it will be done must be addressed. Figure 7.1 identifies the major tasks which must be accomplished during the transition phase of a BPR project.

DETERMINE ALTERNATIVES

Logically there can only be one recommendation from the redesign phase, since the outcome of that phase is to deter-

---

Logical Representation (what)
versus
Physical Representation (how)

Logical Representation	Physical Representation
Outcome of Redesign Phase	Outcome of Transition Phase
Recommendation A	Alternative 1 to Recommendation A
	Alternative 2 to Recommendation A
	Alternative 3 to Recommendation A

Figure 7.2 The outcome of the redesign phase of a BPR project is a logical representation of what should be done. This recommendation is the starting point for the transition phase of the project which may consist of different team members. The outcome of the transition phase of the BPR project is a transitional model or physical representation of how the changes recommended in the redesign phase should be implemented. Usually three alternative implementation solutions are provided. There is a one-too-many relationship between the redesign recommendation and the alternatives identified in the transition phase of the project.

mine what needs to be done. If the redesign phase produces multiple recommendations, then the team has incorporated into their recommendation some of the physical characteristics of how the redesign will be implemented. Figure 7.2 depicts the relationship between a logical representation and a physical one.

The transition team identifies various ways the recommended changes could be implemented. For every recommendation from a redesign team, multiple alternative solutions should be provided. Many of the techniques used in the redesign phase such as brainstorming, JRP sessions, and modeling can be used during the transition phase. It is desirable to identify several alternatives because it forces team members to contemplate alternative implementation methods they might not initially consider. It is generally more difficult to identify more than three alternative solutions. After several alternatives have been identified, they should be evaluated against feasibility and requirements issues established in the redesign phase.

At least three viable alternative solutions to present to senior management should remain. Figure 7.3 provides an example of various implementation solutions for a given redesign recommendation. Of course, more solutions could be recommended; however, the more solutions investigated, the longer the BPR project will take to complete. In other words, a limit must be placed on the number of solutions identified in order to keep the costs of the project down and keep it on schedule.

Strategic Analysis

Various viable alternatives must be identified at this time, maintaining a high level of abstraction. The transition team members need time to fully understand the requirements of the redesigned process. The requirements are those functions that the redesigned process must incorporate in order to interact with existing systems and processes within the organization. At a higher level of abstraction the team members need to understand what the redesigned process will accomplish in order to effectively identify alternative ways of how it could be done. This task is called strategic analysis. During strategic analysis the transition team will spend time analyzing current processes and related data. They will use methods such as interviews, focus groups, observation, forms analysis, and polling.

♦ Interviews are an effective method for obtaining information; however, they are time-consuming.

♦ Focus groups, or group interviews focused on a specific topic, are a useful technique which allow for the greatest amount of information to be gleaned within the shortest amount of time. Focus groups also allow the participants to learn what others are doing and how all the various procedures involved in the redesign project are interrelated.

♦ Observing work procedures is another method analysts use to obtain information during the strategic analysis

Recommendation from redesign phase of BPR project	Alternative from transition phase of BPR project
Combine sales operations between the existing 8 regional offices.	*Alternative 1* Connect all 8 offices together via leased dedicated phone lines and maintain a central database in region x which all offices can dial into.
	Alternative 2 Distribute the sales and marketing data between the 8 regional offices and allow each office access to all of the data. Implement client/server technology to allow transparent access to the data at all 8 locations, simultaneously if necessary. The offices will connect through an Internet services provider and use TCP/IP.
	Alternative 3 Consolidate the 8 offices into one physical location with a central database.

Figure 7.3 This is an example of how three viable alternatives could be generated from a redesign phase recommendation. The outlined alternatives are in no way inclusive. They merely illustrate the fact that more detail is provided in the transition alternatives and the issues may become very technical. In many instances, technology is the enabling force behind redesign projects. However, not all solutions will, or should be, technology-driven. Note that Alternative 3 is not a technical solution to the redesign recommendation.

task. Observation can help provide answers to questions or conflicting procedures uncovered during interviews.

♦ Forms or document analysis is another method that can address data requirements. By ascertaining the current data captured or generated by the existing process, better understanding of what data is required by the redesigned system is obtained.

♦ Polling is the most informal method identified here. However, it is a useful technique, if the process under investigation affects a large number of people in various departments. By polling, or sending questionnaires, better understanding of issues related to the redesigned process can be determined.

These techniques are not all-encompassing, but provide an overview of techniques which can be used to complete the strategic analysis task.

Strategic Design

Strategic design, which is the task immediately following strategic analysis, provides an opportunity for team members to explore implementation possibilities without becoming too detailed. It also allows the team members to brainstorm and think of creative ways to apply technology, as well as consider existing resources, to implement the recommended changes (redesigned process). (See Figure 7.4.) Determining alternatives consists of strategic analysis and design, and addresses issues such as the following:

♦ Are there any portions of the recommendation developed in the redesign phase that could be automated? The redesign could, and usually does, consist of both manual and automated segments.

♦ Are there any new technologies available to simplify the recommendation (redesigned process)?

♦ Is the recommended implementation independent? In other words, could the recommendation (the outcome of the redesign phase), be implemented in various ways (i.e.,

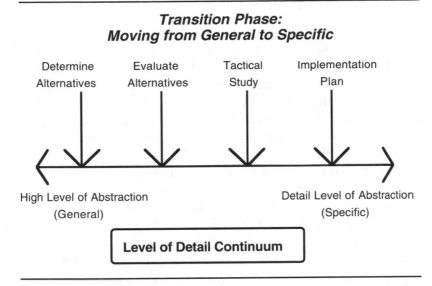

Figure 7.4 As you progress not only from the redesign phase to the transition phase, but also from the beginning of one phase to the end of that phase, you are moving along the level of detail continuum. Initially, information is gathered at a high level of abstraction; as further investigation and analysis is completed, more detailed information is uncovered, captured, and analyzed.

manually, central computer system, distributed computer system, imaging technology, etc.)?

Once strategic or high-level issues are addressed, the feasibility of each alternative can be ascertained. Up to this point in the BPR project, each alternative solution identified has not been developed in explicit detail. Enough information has not been generated to actually implement any of the alternative solutions identified. A great deal of time should not be spent working out all the details of a specific alternative only to discover it either is not a feasible solution or does not meet the requirements established during the redesign phase. Alternative solutions (how to implement the redesigned process) should be identified during the strategic design task of the transition phase. The next task in the transition phase is to evaluate those alternatives.

EVALUATE ALTERNATIVES

Although feasibility was addressed during the planning phase of the BPR project, the level of understanding of the project was limited because a great deal of detail was not identified. Therefore, feasibility was addressed at a higher, more theoretical level during the redesign phase. The issue of feasibility must be addressed again for each alternative solution proposed. During the transition phase, feasibility is addressed for each alternative solution based on the redesign team's recommended process changes. Because analyzing the feasibility of each alternative solution is time-consuming, the number of viable solutions investigated should be kept at a manageable number, between 5 and 10.

It is much easier to deal with feasibility issues during the transition phase than during the planning or redesign phases. The issues addressed during the transition phase relate to specific technologies, and specific changes in procedures, organizational structure, or personnel assignments. It is much easier to determine whether senior management will support a change when the change is specific rather than general. For instance, it is easier to determine whether it is technically feasible to connect 200 computers in seven regional offices when you know exactly how many computers there are, the distance between them, the operating systems they are running under, and the internetworking protocols they will be using. It is much harder to determine if a recommendation is technically feasible when the only request you have is that data must be electronically shared between the regional offices—the level of detail available during the redesign phase. Because more detail has been identified during strategic analysis and design tasks, the feasibility issue must be revisited at a more specific level. At this point in the BPR project the following steps should have been completed:

♦ Redesign phase has recommended what the new process or system should do and has been approved by senior management.
♦ The transition team has been formed; some members

may have remained the same, others may have been added or removed. (Tactical Planning for Transition Phase, end of Redesign Phase)

- ◆ The transition team has determined between 5 and 10 alternative solutions to the recommendation proposed by the redesign team. (Strategic Design Task)
- ◆ The transition team has evaluated each of the alternative solutions for technical, economic, and political feasibility. The number of viable solutions was probably reduced. (Evaluate Alternatives Task)

Evaluate Solutions against Requirements

Now the identified alternative solutions should be evaluated according to the requirements established during the redesign phase of the project. The requirements identified in the redesign phase distinguished between mandatory and optional or desirable features. At this point in the project any feasible alternatives should be reevaluated according to these requirements. If any requirements which were identified as mandatory create debate among the transition team members, a joint requirements planning (JRP) type of session should be held with all of the redesign team and transition team members in order to ensure the requirements specified are properly interpreted. A discussion may ensue regarding why certain items were identified as mandatory rather than optional. The issue of whether a requirement should be classified as mandatory or optional may be reopened at this time. As long as the members of both teams agree, this is acceptable. In fact, it is a good sign if questioning, probing, and creative thinking are going on during this task. Just as some of the alternatives may have been eliminated during the feasibility evaluation, some may also be excluded during requirements evaluation.

If more than three or four alternatives remain, the transition team should examine the optional criteria and select the best three or four solutions to be forwarded to senior management for approval to continue. Senior management would not be able to choose a solution at this time because further investigation into each proposed alternative solution must be completed. However, having a preliminary checkpoint at this time is valuable. It ensures that the transition team is evaluating the solutions against realistic criteria. For example, the team may assume that certain technologies, such as client/server technology, will not be accepted by senior management and staff. However, if there is feedback to management at this point, then the opportunity exists for this misleading assumption to be rectified and the team may add or change one of the alternative solutions they are evaluating accordingly. Once there is assurance that the team is "on the right track," they can then move to tactical study tasks.

TACTICAL STUDY

The tactical study task addresses the details involved in determining not only *what*, but *how* each alternative solution should be implemented. During this portion of the transition phase, the technical team members will be doing most of the work. Issues considered for each alternative solution proposed include such items as the following:

♦ If portions of the redesigned project will be automated, what hardware platforms will they exist on? Will new hardware and/or operating systems need to be purchased?

♦ If part of the redesign includes custom development, what programming languages will be used?

♦ If a database will support the corporate information, which one will be used?

♦ If policies will be changed, are there any legal ramifications?

♦ If personnel responsibilities will change, are there any union issues that need to be resolved?

The tactical study of a BPR project can be compared to the detailed analysis and the high-level design of a structured analysis project. Figure 7.5 shows the major tasks in-

BPR Project Phases & Tasks	When traditional systems development tasks would occur in relationship to a BPR project
Planning Phase ♦ Scope ♦ Feasibility ♦ Benefit	Information strategic planning
Redesign Phase ♦ Problem Identification ♦ Requirements Definition ♦ Redesign Process ♦ Recommendation	Business area analysis
Transition Phase ♦ Determine Alternatives ♦ Evaluate Alternatives ♦ Tactical Study ♦ Implementation Plan	Feasibility study Analysis Design System Proposal
Implementation Phase ♦ Project Management ♦ Change Management ♦ Assessment	Hardware/Software installation Programming User training Customer sign off

Figure 7.5 This table shows the tasks of a BPR project and when traditional systems development tasks such as programming would be undertaken. The phases of the BPR project do not directly correlate with the phases of a structured analysis project.

volved in a structured analysis project, including when they would be accomplished with respect to a BPR project. Most of the traditional systems development process occurs during the transition and implementation phases of a BPR project. The planning and redesign phases are more involved with the business aspects of the project. Structured analysis or information systems development projects do not generally address these issues; they are more concerned with implementing the technical solution.

A benefit of combining traditional systems development with the BPR project is that all areas of the organization are focused on the same issue. Separate groups are not trying to obtain the same goals from different directions; therefore, redundancy within the organization is greatly reduced. In many organizations various business units embark on total quality management or process improvement initiatives while the information systems department is working on information engineering or systems development projects to automate existing processes. The initiatives of these two groups may overlap. By combining the efforts of BPR and systems development into a larger, more broad methodology for changing processes within the organization, cooperation and synergy will exist.

Solutions Proposal

The outcome or document which is generated from the tactical study is the solutions proposal. This document outlines each of the alternative solutions previously identified, along with detailed information regarding the implementation of each one. Of course, the document should identify which alternative the team recommends. However, it should also be given to senior management in order for them to select which alternative solution they want implemented. The reason behind allowing senior management to select the alternative is their ability to see the "big picture." In other words, extenuating circumstances may exist concerning why a particular alternative is not appealing to the organization at this time. The members of the transition team may not be privy to this type of information. (Senior management does not usually participate actively in the transition phase of a project.)

Depending on the type of BPR project undertaken, the level of detail desired during the tactical study will vary. If a major portion of the redesigned process will be automated and complex information systems will be purchased, developed in-house, or integrated with off-the-shelf software, then detailed systems specifications will be necessary. If, however, a software package along with some manual procedural changes will accomplish the recommended redesign, the level of detail necessary in tactical analysis will be less. In this case it is extremely helpful to use data flow diagrams and entity-relationship diagrams developed during the redesign phase. It saves a great deal of work on the part of the computer systems developers to be able to use models previously developed. If technology will play a major role in implementing the redesigned changes, which it often does, then detailed specifications for database design as well as program logic is necessary.

Depending on the size of the project, computer-aided software engineering (CASE) tools may be required. The models developed in the redesign phase will need to be imported into the CASE tool that the systems developers will be working on, if it has not already been done. A CASE tool may capture the information gathered in the redesign phase, but a technical person should be assigned to input this information into the CASE tool. CASE tools are more powerful and more complex than graphical drawing tools. This power is needed when it comes to developing complex computer information systems. This power is not necessary in the redesign phase; however, it may be necessary in the transition phase.

Just as the necessity for a process was questioned during the redesign phase, the in-house development of systems should be questioned at this time. It is important to question why a system should be developed in-house. There is a tendency, especially within information systems departments, to believe that no system will be able to meet the needs of the organization unless it is developed in-house. After a great deal of time has been spent on redesigning the underlying business process, effort should be spent to ensure that time-consuming systems are not developed in-house unnecessarily. The probing technique described in Appendix A and used during the redesign phase to help individuals break through barriers when redesigning processes would be useful at this time as well. Again, it is imperative to question why a system must be developed in-house. In many instances, commercial software is available that can meet the needs of the redesigned processes or integrating various software packages may solve the problem. Breakthrough thinking must occur when designing how the new process will be implemented as well as when deciding what the process should do in the first place.

TACTICAL PLANNING FOR IMPLEMENTATION PHASE

After senior management determines which alternative they want implemented, an implementation plan must be developed. Depending on the solution selected by senior management, various issues will need to be considered. However, there may be a substantial gap in time between providing the solutions and working on the implementation plan. Since many of the team members will change between these two phases, individuals will not be waiting for approval to move forward. For those individuals who will remain on the team, this gap between phases allows them time to work on their regular duties or on another BPR project.

Once the decision by senior management has been made, the implementation planning process should move forward. This task is included in the transition phase because the transition team members determine the composition of the implementation team. The team leader will still be involved throughout implementation; however, most of the other team members will disperse at this time. The skills and expertise required at the implementation phase are very different from the redesign and transition phases. During the redesign phase, desirable skills are abstract thinking, risk-taking, and creativity. During the transition phase, desirable skills include technological awareness, sequential thinking, and the ability to conceptualize models. During the implementation phase, skills necessary to implement changes include programming, and attention to detail from the technical participants. From other team members, skills such as empathy, diplomacy, and various people skills are necessary to help the staff overcome the fear of change.

During implementation planning, the following types of issues are addressed:

♦   Who will develop training materials for staff?
♦   How will the change be introduced to the staff?
♦   Will policy or procedure be rewritten?
♦   Does the programming staff need any retraining in order to implement the recommended solution?

At this time, the team members for the next phase as well as the resources needed are identified. The actual implementation plan is developed during the implementation phase. Forethought should also be given to time lines for the implementation phase.

Training Issues

The successful training or retraining of staff is an integral part of the successful implementation of a redesigned process. Training is important, not only for end users or departmental staff, but also for technical staff. Training budgets are one aspect of the BPR project that should not be cut back if funding is an issue. After all the time, effort, and money has been spent to redesign the business process, if people are not knowledgeable about the changes and how they will affect them, the entire project will not be successful. Training, in the sense it is used here, is much more than learning new keystrokes on a software package. Training includes helping staff obtain the skill sets they will need in order to perform a role in the redesigned process. In many cases, the redesign will drastically change what they have been doing, especially if technology is applied to the redesigned processes. Staff will need to understand what their new responsibilities are and how the changes will affect them personally.

Training issues can be incorporated with the process of gathering support for the changes—the buy-in process. Senior management, middle management, and supervisors must support the changes in order for the project to be successful. If staff are receiving mixed messages from the management team, it will be difficult to obtain their support for the change. It is necessary to have everyone support the changes and pull in one direction. Inertia is a powerful force. If changes are not supported by all levels of management, the temptation to revert to the old way of doing things is overwhelming.

JIT Training

If internal staff does not possess the necessary skills, outside consultants are required; this provides a good opportunity to train your internal staff for the next BPR project. Outside consultants can also serve as overseers, ensuring the project is kept on target. Internal resistors to change and negative input can be kept in check by someone whose expertise includes current knowledge of technologies as well as BPR techniques. Using the concepts of JIT training, internal staff can be assigned to work with an expert outside consultant in order to learn specific techniques. If a new technology will be implemented, the internal staff members' training can be augmented by a formal class. However, if any staff members will be sent to formal training, you want to ensure that they use their newly acquired skills immediately or they will be lost. Without practice, new skill sets will not be retained. Because of this lack of retention, JIT training is an attractive alternative to formal classroom training. However, combining both JIT training with formal classroom instruction in a timely manner will provide the quickest and longest lasting retention of new skills.

Cross-Training

Cross-training is another concept that should be considered. If your organization has a few people versed in BPR techniques as well as implementing new technologies, you want to leverage their expertise. Rather than hiring an outside consultant to work with internal staff, use your existing in-

ternal experts to work with others within your company—
sharing the internal knowledge base. Some of the benefits of
cross-training are outlined below.

♦ The more skills your employees possess, the more versa-
tile they will become—able to work on various phases of
BPR projects.

♦ If a person has to be reassigned or terminated due to the
BPR project, the extra skills learned will be helpful in
placing the person in a new position.

♦ Continually training and expanding the horizons of your
staff will benefit not only the employee, but also the
organization.

Reengineering should not create new static processes
which will become ingrained in the future history of the organization. Continual improvement and change should be built-
in to any changes currently being contemplated. Because a
redesigned process should continually improve and mature,
well-trained team members will be vital to successful future
changes of the current BPR project, as well as to implementing and continually improving other redesign projects.

Change Management Issues

While documenting manual procedural changes and implementing technical aspects of the redesigned process, it is
important to remember that the main focus of the BPR
implementation project should be on facilitating change. If
major changes are to be introduced, the staff must be prepared to accept them. It has been proven through implementing computer information systems, that if end users do
not like the system, they will not use it. The most effective
computer system could be developed, but if the end user
does not feel comfortable with it, implementation will not be
successful. The same holds true for any BPR project. In fact,
the tendency to reject the solution is probably greater because changes are generally more radical. If people resist
automating manual processes, how much more resistant will

they be to radically changing those processes? Because of the nature of these issues, team members dealing with facilitating the change must have certain characteristics.

♦ They must be empathetic to employees' needs.
♦ They need to be diplomatic while encouraging acceptance of the proposed changes.
♦ They must be capable of internally marketing the changes.

Team members must be selected who not only possess the skills necessary to accomplish these tasks, but who are also in a position to demand respect. This may mean that they have line authority over a particular area or, through the informal chain of command, they are well respected by the staff. In effect, the membership of the team is diverse, requiring people skills as well as technical skills. It is not realistic to assume that one person can serve in all of these roles; therefore, several people will be required who possess the needed skills. The implementation team will actually consist of several subteams (subteam structure will be explained in detail in Chapter 8).

♦ Manual Procedure Changes Subteam
♦ Technical Implementation Subteam
♦ Change Facilitation Subteam

In the development of traditional information systems, the human factor was often left unaddressed. Recently computer systems development methodologies, such as STRADIS, have incorporated the human factor into the development process. Emphasis was placed on designing computer system interfaces which were not only functional but also appealing to the computer user. Manual processes were included as part of the computer system development methodology; however, the issue of *facilitating change* was still left unaddressed. Traditionally, change management issues were outside the realm of computer systems development. BPR projects incorporate the traditional computer systems development into a larger project that addresses what the organization should

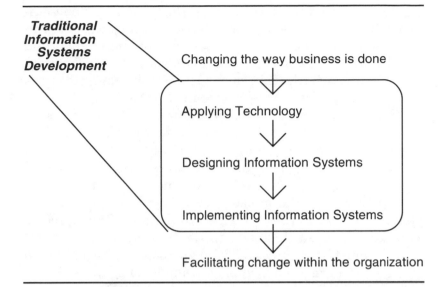

Figure 7.6 Reengineering incorporates some of the functions that traditional information systems development contains. Traditional information systems development can be viewed as a subset of a business reengineering project. It is accomplished during the transition and implementation phases of the business reengineering project. Technology plays a major role in implementing redesigned processes in many cases; however, changing the way business is done—redesigning the underlying business processes needs to be done before any technology solutions are applied. Because of the changing focus of the project throughout the BPR effort, the team composition also must change.

do, how it will be done, and how to facilitate those changes. Figure 7.6 graphically represents this concept.

Policy and Procedure Issues

The changes recommended during the redesign phase and the specific solution associated with that recommendation proposed during the transition phase may affect procedures or policies of the organization. Planning must include these issues. If procedure manuals need to be rewritten, this must be incorporated into the implementation plan. By identifying the tasks that will be completed during the implementation phase of the project, a list of possible team members can be drafted. Depending on the severity of the change and whether any personnel will lose their jobs or require retraining in another skill, team members with human resources or change management expertise may be required.

Changes to the manual procedures will be necessary whether any technology is applied to the redesigned project. In some instances an entire process may be eliminated, in which case existing procedures or processes that are affected by the eliminated process will need to be altered. During the redesign phase of the project, identification of processes or procedures which are interrelated to the redesigned process were identified. At this point in the project, the procedural changes must be documented, and any policy changes should be adjusted in manuals, employee handbooks, and so forth. The specific details targeting which documents require change, as well as which procedures need to be updated and distributed to staff should be determined by the implementation team during their planning tasks. The actual plan to document these changes is not developed until the next phase. However, it is important to know what needs to be accomplished during the next phase in order to identify team members and plan time lines.

The team members involved in implementing the manual procedure changes should be well-versed in corporate politics, as well as familiar with the business processes being redesigned. It is also desirable if they are not attached to current policies and procedures, but aware of them, so that they know what changes will need to be made. Team members involved in this portion of the implementation should be very detail-oriented and able to communicate well, both orally and in writing, in order to effectively document the changes.

Technical Issues

Planning for the technical issues during implementation includes the following:

♦ Determine what type of training will be required for internal technical staff, if technical issues need to be resolved.

♦ Ascertain whether outside programmers, consultants, systems integrators, or other technical experts will be required.

♦ Determine if software and hardware will be needed so that the appropriate individuals can work on developing the time line during the implementation phase. (Specific hardware and software questions regarding the time frame for ordering equipment are not addressed at this time; they are resolved during the implementation phase.)

♦ Decide who will be on the team and what major issues they will need to address.

♦ Determine hardware requirements.

CHAPTER HIGHLIGHTS

✎ The transition phase of a BPR project can contain traditional systems development projects. The redesign phase provides a recommendation for redesign which is the starting point of the transition phase.

✎ The alternative solutions identified will invariably be technology-based. Technology is an enabling force allowing many of the business process redesign initiatives to take place. However, a person should be careful not to look to technology as the only solution, especially in-house customized programming.

✎ Many changes can be affected with limited or existing technologies, depending on the scope of the project and the breadth of the changes involved. Just as you want to focus on shifting paradigms when redesigning business processes, you want to focus on innovative ways to implement those changes. Technology is changing and computer programming is changing. Client/server technology, end-user computing, and distributed databases allow for creative and innovative technical solutions to recommended business process changes.

✎ Technology should not drive the change. This is one reason why the redesign phase is separated from the transition phase. *It allows you to focus on the business issues separate from the technical issues.*

✎ At least three alternative solutions should be identified. It is more difficult to identify multiple solutions. The benefits, however, include more creative solutions.

✎ Strategic analysis involves understanding what the redesigned process should accomplish at a higher level of abstraction. It does not delve into a great deal of detail. The documentation produced by the redesign phase outlining what the redesigned process should accomplish is an excellent source of material for strategic analysis.

✎ There are several different techniques used to help determine how the recommended system could be developed. These techniques can also be used in any of the phases of the project to gather information.
   ◊ Interviewing
   ◊ Focus Groups
   ◊ Observation
   ◊ Forms or Document Analysis
   ◊ Polling

✎ The strategic design task allows team members to explore possible alternative solutions to the recommended redesign without becoming too detailed. Alternatives and possibilities explored during this task may not be viable; however, they may spark an idea that blossoms into a great solution.

✎ The solutions proposal is the document generated from the tactical study task of the transition phase of the business reengineering project. It addresses how the specified recommendation identified in the redesign phase should be implemented. This must be accomplished before planning for the implementation phase can begin.

✎ Training is an important part of any project. If processes have been redesigned, and portions automated, training must consist of both the manual and automated changes in the redesigned process.

✎ Training should occur not only for departmental staff, but also for technical staff. If the technology infrastructure changes in order to accommodate the redesigned process, the technical staff will need to be retrained.

✎ JIT training is a viable and preferred alternative to traditional workshop or classroom training. It is similar to the concept of on-the-job training; however, equal emphasize should be placed between *doing* and *learning*.

✎ Cross-training is another concept that should be incorporated into an implementation plan.

Implementation Phase

After processes have been redesigned and solutions for implementing change have been identified, the changes must be made. Though this may seem simple, this is the phase of the project that will provide the most challenges and require the most varied skill set. Figure 8.1 provides an overview of the steps involved in the implementation phase of a business reengineering project. In order to accommodate the need for a varied skill set, team members should be selected from various functional areas of the organization, or outside consultants, who would augment the internal staff's skill set, should be retained. The composition of the implementation team, as well as the challenges facing such as team, will be discussed in this chapter. The implementation team is actually three subteams, each with its own required skill sets. Figure 8.2 illustrates the focus of each subteam within the implementation team. However, before discussing the team composition, it is important to understand issues affecting implementation and the selection of team members.

ISSUES AFFECTING IMPLEMENTATION

There are certain issues, other than team selection, that will directly affect the success of implementation. Personnel, as

Business Reengineering Guidelines Implementation Phase	
BPR Phases	**Tasks within phases**
Planning	see Chapter 5
Redesign	see Chapter 6
Transition	see Chapter 7
Implementation	Develop an Understanding of Issues Affecting Implementation
	Refine Implementation Plan
	♦ Identify specific tasks to be accomplished
	♦ Identify team members' roles
	♦ Determine deadlines and milestones
	♦ Determine resources required
	♦ Differential manual and automated processes
	Develop Testing Plan
	Develop Training Plan
	Implement Manual and Automated Portions Concurrently
	Test Automated Portions
	Train Staff
	Assess Implemented Redesigned Process

Figure 8.1 The tasks outlined provide a guideline for a business reengineering project. These guidelines can be modified to accommodate any scope business reengineering project (enterprise reengineering, business process redesign (BPR), work-flow analysis, and technology applications). However, this information must be customized by each organization in order to be effective.

well as cultural issues within the organization will directly affect success. Some corporate cultures are based on lengthy history and years of tradition. For those organizations, change will be more difficult. Even newer companies have a

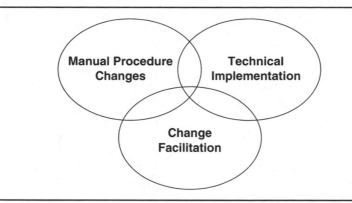

Figure 8.2 The implementation team actually consists of three distinct subteams which need to work effectively together in order to ensure the successful implementation of the BPR project. Different skills are required for each of the team facets. Traditionally, technical implementation was the implementation team. With the advent of information engineering concepts manual procedure changes were also addressed. Business reengineering projects, however, focus not only on the manual and automated changes, but also on how to implement those changes—change management issues addressed by a change facilitation implementation subteam.

corporate culture which must be taken into account. Even though it is not ingrained in procedures and policies, the personal values and morals of the founders of the company set the tone for the culture of the organization. Personnel considerations, other than those for selecting the team, must be taken into account as well.

Personnel Considerations

Senior management's role in implementing the proposed redesigned processes is important. It is directly affected by their management style. Most organizations foster a certain type of management style in their senior executives. This relates to the culture of the organization and what is viewed as acceptable behavior. Managers who practice Douglas McGregor's Theory Y and participative management, which gained momentum during the 1980s, have the type of environment conducive to change (see Figure 8.3).

Motivational Theory Summarization	
Theory X	*Theory Y*
The main presumption of Theory X is that employees are passive, even resistant, to organizational needs. They need constant supervision in order to accomplish any tasks because they are basically irresponsible.	The main presumption of Theory Y is that employees are not irresponsible or lazy. Given the opportunity to align their personal goals with the organization's will provide internal motivation. People do not need to be continually told what to do and how to do it.

Figure 8.3 Douglas McGregor's motivational theory is summarized here. The theory that management in an organization adheres to either Theory X or Theory Y greatly affects how change will be handled within that organization. If management believes Theory X, the changes will be kept secret until implementation, at which time a dictatorial posture will be taken.

♦ The best environment, and ultimately the best senior management support, is one of trust and respect.
  ◊ If senior management hold the philosophy that employees want to do a good job, given the opportunity, then change can be introduced as a positive result.
  ◊ On the other hand, if senior management's role is a dictatorial one in which all changes are kept secretive until decisions have been made, the role of the BPR implementation team is made more difficult.
♦ Attitudes of senior management must be addressed in order to implement change. The management philosophy of executives is directly related to the successful implementation of any change.

If risk-taking is encouraged, if management views employees as vital participants in achieving the goals of the organization, then introducing any redesigned processes will be easier.

Middle management, as well as senior management, plays a vital role in successful implementation. Today, the trend in many organizations is to reduce the number of middle managers. This downsizing has been targeted at more middle managers than frontline supervisors or senior executives. Therefore, the implementation team should be aware of middle management's perceived and sometimes real threat of business process changes.

♦ Technology has played a vital role in changing the function of middle management. In the past, middle management's main purpose was to filter information to top management, summarizing information and data gathered by the daily operations of the organization. Executive information systems (EIS) and database query tools have eliminated the need for this function in many organizations.

♦ Another role middle management played was disseminating information from senior management to the appropriate staff. However, with electronic mail and electronic bulletin board systems, information can be disseminated throughout an organization and beyond more quickly and more effectively. This middle management role of summarizing and disseminating information is no longer needed. Consequently, the role of middle management is being redefined.

In many cases, layers of management are being eliminated in order to streamline the organization. This is a good example of how technologies, as outlined in Appendix B, have enabled changes in business processes to occur. The technologies of electronic mail and groupware have allowed corporations to rethink the roles of middle management. Because of this growing trend toward a flatter organizational structure, middle management will be apprehensive about changing processes, especially within their functional areas of responsibility. Major changes in the processes for which middle management is responsible equate to major changes in middle management's responsibilities. There is also the possibility that specific departments and their associated processes will be merged, outsourced, or eliminated altogether. In order for the implementation to be successful the level of management directly responsible for the changes must be involved in implementation. The level of management that is responsible will vary depending on the project. This is definitely a challenge for the implementation team, especially when those managers directly involved in the process have the most at stake. Advocates from all levels of management, however, must be involved in implementing the changes in order to ensure success.

Senior and middle management's roles also include advocating changes and providing an atmosphere in which change is encouraged. However, staff play a very vital role in the implementation of a BPR project as well. If staff involved in the redesigned process does not accept the changes, there will be resistance. Resistance from staff can take many forms, ranging from complaining about the changes and the redesigned process, to outright sabotage of those changes. In most instances, sabotage would not be an alternative; however, there are many ways a change can be undermined.

For instance, in the past, when computer information systems were developed and implemented in the end users' offices, people would often refuse to use the system—maintaining their manual procedures. Or, if they were forced to use the system, they would forget to enter pertinent data because they were maintaining a separate manual system which they relied upon for information and did not need the new computer system. Very few employees would be so resistant to change that they would sabotage the redesigned process on purpose. However, problems may unintentionally arise.

If the staff involved in day-to-day operations continually "forget" to follow certain procedures which have been changed, the success of the project can be jeopardized. Change is difficult, especially when people don't understand how the change will affect them. It is the responsibility of the implementation team focusing on *facilitating change* to help individuals overcome their fear of change and illustrate how the change will favorably affect them.

Most of the time resistance to change takes the form of protesting the change. Employees resistant to change will find myriad reasons why the redesigned process will not work. So, it is important for the team to determine who the resistors will be and solicit their input early in the implementation phase. In this way, you can not only determine what factors of the redesigned process may cause concern, but also provide an opportunity for people to think about the changes before they occur. If staff who are also resistors play an integral part in the redesigned process, then their involvement should begin during the transition phase.

If resistors can be identified early in the BPR project, there are several ways to turn a possible negative aspect of implementation into a positive one. Once those resistant to change have been identified, whether they are senior management, middle management, or staff, half the battle is won. Implementation team members working on facilitating change can begin to enlist the assistance of identified resistors. People are resistant to change because they do not see any benefit in the change for themselves or for their goals. If they can see that the redesigned process will provide them with some type of benefit, then there is a possibility for them to become advocates of the change. For example, if the change involves reorganizing an IS department and certain computer pro grammers may be decentralized to various departments to support specific end users and their applications, they may view this as a stifling change. However, if because of this change they will learn more about the business operation, and ultimately be better positioned to move into an analysts' position, then they should be made aware of this.

♦ A negative change aspect should be turned into a positive benefit for individuals resistant to change or anyone for that matter.
♦ Whenever a negative aspect of the change is identified, question why this is a negative aspect.
♦ Ask yourself how you can turn the situation around to provide a benefit.

The idea of changing a negative aspect into a positive one can be used not only with people resistant to change, but also to help introduce the change in a more favorable light.

An episode of "Star Trek, The Next Generation" illustrates this point superbly. A mediator was sent to negotiate peace between two warring factions on a distant planet. The negotiator could not speak any language; he was mute. Several interpreters traveled with him. This was his asset—he could communicate with various peoples through his interpreters. A major change occurred; through an accident he lost his interpreters—this change was definitely viewed as negative. How could he negotiate a peace settlement when he could not communicate with the two warring factions? The underlying theme of that particular episode was to turn a negative change into a positive one. After perceiving the situation in a different light, the loss of his interpreters became a positive change. He used his inability to communicate as a means for gaining trust and ultimately the understanding of each faction. He decided that the two warring factions, as well as himself, would spend a great deal of time learning sign language in order to communicate. In this way, all parties were learning to trust each other. Once they learned enough sign language to communicate with each other, they would be more apt to listen to each other because they had built a relationship and learned to communicate. With some people, implementing change may feel like communicating with aliens on distant planets; however, the idea of taking negative changes and seeking positive benefits is an important concept that directly relates to facilitating changes brought about by redesigned business processes.

Corporate Culture

The role of various levels of personnel in changing existing processes has been explored. During that discussion, the issue of corporate culture was raised. The corporate culture of an organization can be thought of as the conglomerate of its management's values and morals. The culture of the organization is generally set by the founders of the institution. Thus the older the company, the deeper the culture is embedded into policies and procedures. Because of this, many new companies have been successful implementing new procedures and processes. Newer companies are able to adapt to changes in the environment, foreign trade pressures, and government deregulation more quickly since they don't rely on past traditions and a deeply ingrained corporate culture to guide their thinking. The culture initially formed by the founders is enhanced by the subsequent generations of senior management staffs.

Generally, most organizations that have existed for more than 20 years will have retained military mannerisms in their corporate culture, basically because management styles of senior staff have included military aspects. Most senior executives 20 or more years ago served in the military before joining the corporate ranks. In fact, the basic model upon which most organizations are built is a military, hierarchical model. This model is based on authority by position and the unwritten rule that the chain of command cannot be broken—in other words, you never would go to a superior's counterpart in another department if you had an idea. All ideas and communications are funneled through the lines of command, something that electronic mail and electronic bulletin boards are eroding.

This model was a fertile ground for developing layer upon layer of management, since the only way to increase one's authority or reward someone's good work within the organization was through a line promotion. Many organizations have 10 or 15 levels of management within their organizations. Some even have more! Imagine the amount of filtering done by each level. Is it a wonder why very little change occurs in large organizations? By the time the information reaches senior management, if it reaches them at all, the meaning of the message is most often lost. The same holds true for information flowing in the other direction. By the time the staff receive word of a change, it has been filtered and altered by so many layers of management that it is hard to discern the true meaning of the initial message.

Most people have played the children's game where a line is formed—the longer the better—and the first child whispers a secret a few sentences long into the next child's ear. The secret message is passed from child to child until it reaches the end of the line. When the last child in line hears the message he announces out loud what the message was. The first child then corrects him by repeating the initial message. The message is never the same. Everyone laughs at how the message has become twisted because each child has filtered the message. They try to remember the exact message; however, each of us has our own background and experiences we bring to whatever we do. We all hear and interpret communications differently. Is it any wonder why senior management is amazed that certain directives have not been followed through or that different departments seem to be going in different directions. Many organizations' communications channels have unintentionally been modeled after this children's game. When all communications must go through the chain of command, is it really any different than an adult version of the children's telephone game?

Business process redesign efforts are directly affected by the culture. By attempting to change the way business is done, and in the case of reengineering projects, the essence or mission of the business itself, conflict with the existing culture is often certain. Part of the BPR project's implementation task is to overcome existing corporate cultural barriers to change. For instance, some organizations, especially educational institutions, have rewarded longevity. Primarily because the administrative side of educational institutions is modeled by its academic counterparts, tenure is ingrained firmly in the culture. Most educational institutions have awards for length of service and recognition is given to those who have been part of the *history* and *tradition* of the institution. However, just as the private sector is facing change, the educational sector is as well. Higher education, in particular, is in the midst of rethinking its role and how it provides education to its customers (students). With all of these changes occurring, the administration in many schools is starting to downplay the importance of longevity. It is finding that bringing in new people, with new ideas, is what is needed in order to stay competitive. This is a major shift in the culture and one that is difficult for individuals to accept, especially if they have been with the institution for 10 or more years and have become entrenched in the culture where longevity is rewarded. When the shift in the corporate culture occurs, such as when longevity is no longer desired, individuals experience a form of culture shock.

Inertia, doing things the same way, is also difficult to overcome. Personnel at all levels in the organization must overcome the tendency to hold onto the old way of doing things. The more radical the proposed change, the more difficult the acceptance of that change. The implementation team must be aware that: *People do not resist change because they want to be difficult; they resist change because they are afraid of the unknown.*

Everyone has experienced this trepidation at some point in their lives. Whenever people move to a new city or leave an existing position, for example, they feel anticipation as well as anxiety. It is always easier to remain static. The same holds true for change within the organization. People become comfortable with procedures, with knowing what needs to be done, and with doing it in the same way. Once you are aware that the reason people resist change is basically fear of the unknown, you can plan accordingly. If people are kept informed about what the proposed changes are, and know how they will be implemented, much of their anxiety will be alleviated. In essence the job of introducing the change will be easier. Taking into account corporate culture as well as personnel issues, the implementation of the redesigned process can begin.

IMPLEMENTING THE SOLUTION—"DO IT"

Figure 8.1 outlines the major tasks required during the implementation phase. Again, these tasks are only suggestions; an implementation plan, starting with these suggestions, should be developed, but may be modified. The implementation phase of the BPR project is the one that requires the most tenacity and determination. Talking about changing procedures, even about allocating funding to investigate the possibility, is not the same as actually implementing those changes. This is one reason why the first BPR project undertaken by an organization should have a scope that is small enough to allow for successful implementation while being large enough to ensure a substantial benefit. A strategic or high-level implementation plan as well as identification of key team members should have been developed at the end of the transition phase. This plan serves as the starting point for the implementation phase.

Implementation Team

The implementation team was initially identified at the end of the transition phase. Most of the team members will change when implementation of the redesigned process begins. However, that does not mean the individuals working on the project, especially departmental management, are not still involved in facilitating the changes. Management's roles throughout the BPR project are to help staff feel comfortable with a changing environment and to enlist their assistance in bringing about the changes.

Identifying Subteams for Implementation Purposes

The composition of the implementation team will depend heavily upon the redesign solution adopted by senior management. If the redesigned process will be implemented extensively using technologies, then the team will consist primarily of technical experts as well as individuals familiar with change management issues. The implementation team will consist of three distinct groups who will rely upon each other for the successful implementation of the project—manual procedure changes, technical implementation, and change facilitation. Depending upon the size of the organization, team members may play more than one role in the implementation—crossing the subteam categories identified in Figure 8.2.

Members of the subteam involved in the technical implementation require the technical expertise necessary to implement the changes. If the redesigned process will be implemented using *client/server* technology and the internal IS staff is only familiar with *mainframe* programming (COBOL for example), a training issue needs to be addressed. Whatever the technology to be applied, team members should be chosen for either their knowledge of that technology or their ability to quickly adapt and learn new skills. Team members will focus on the technical issues of making the redesigned process work. Continuous communication between subteams is required in order to ensure that the progress of the implementation as a whole is not only on track, but also moving in the same direction. Many people who possess technical skills required by the technical implementation subteam also have the tendency to become engrossed in the technical aspects of the implementation to the exclusion of all other issues. The team leader must possess the skills to keep the technical gurus, who are valuable players during the implementation phase, working toward the overall goal of implementing the redesigned process. This provides a challenge to the project leader who must maintain the focus of the entire BPR project, while keeping technical issues in their proper perspective.

Fine-tuning the Implementation Plan

An initial implementation plan was developed during the transition phase in order to identify the composition of key team members. However, that plan was not developed in enough detail in order for the implementation team to proceed. Specific steps within the scope of each of the major tasks identified by the transition team must be completed, so the initial plan that was received from the transition team is basically an outline. It provides the overall direction that the implementation team needs to ensure they are completing the necessary tasks; however, it does not contain enough specific information. The implementation team also assigns team members to specific tasks and possibly adds additional team members after the details of the plan have been identified. The time frame suggested by the transition team should be just that, a suggestion. After greater detail is uncovered, the time frame of the implementation may require adjustment.

Previously discussed personnel issues must be taken into account when the detailed implementation plan is developed. Attention should be given to developing a plan that will work within a given corporate culture. For instance, if tradition is an important aspect of an organization's culture, this fact should be noted, and additional steps should be built into the implementation plan to address this issue. Focus groups may be introduced to discuss the changes and how they will affect individual workers. An open forum similar to governmental town hall meetings may be instituted to help alleviate anxiety and keep everyone informed of changes. Since people are usually resistant to change because they are not sure how changes will affect them, keeping the lines of communication open is critical.

Before specific tasks are identified, it is imperative to differentiate between automated and manual changes. Certain aspects of the redesigned process will be implemented through the utilization of specific technologies; however, other portions will be implemented through manual procedural or policy changes. Two different subteams will work on the manual and automated portions of the change. By identifying, up front, which portions are manual and which are automated, the assignment of specific personnel is easier. In the past most changes introduced through a computer systems development project involved automating routine work rather than augmenting creative work. In other words tasks performed by clerical or support staff or production employees, or repeatable tasks were automated.

Many of the changes involved in a redesign project affect nonroutine work or management's responsibilities directly. Technologies are being applied to internal communications and nonrepetitive tasks such as "what if" analysis and ad hoc information queries. Because of the types of employees affected by the change, the implementation plan will require different tasks than implementation plans to automate routine tasks traditionally undertaken by computer systems development staff.

When computer systems were first implemented, the focus was on ensuring that the technology worked properly and that employees were able to use the system. Training was focused on how to maneuver through screens of the application and what keystrokes to press. When implementing solutions to creative, or nonrepetitive work, the focus of training and support is shifted from how to use the application to what data is available and what it represents. It is more important for the users, not only support staff but management as well, to understand the reasons for change and the capability of any software installed. It must be presumed that whatever is redesigned today will be obsolete within a short time. Therefore, continuous improvement of the redesign system must follow in order for any long-lasting benefit to be derived. Redesigned systems must be established as an on-going process capable of sustaining itself and allowing for continual improvement and modification.

All of these issues should be incorporated into the implementation plan. Various project management software may be useful at this point to keep track of specific tasks, team members allocated to those tasks, and time lines. The detailed implementation plan should consist of the following:

♦ Identification of specific tasks within the implementation plan such as purchase equipment, conduct town hall meetings, write programs, document procedural changes to specific policies and procedures, schedule training sessions, etc.
   ◊ Differentiation between manual and automated implementation tasks should be identified at this point since the manual and automated implementation tasks can be accomplished concurrently by different team members.
   ◊ Personnel and corporate culture issues should be incorporated into the tasks.
   ◊ Implementation tasks should include testing, training, and assessment activities. As much feedback from staff prior to developing the training plan should be obtained so that people's concerns and is-

sues will be addressed during training. The only way to determine those concerns is to talk with the individuals who will require training.

♦ Assignment of team members to specific roles or tasks. For instance, if a team member is well-versed in policies and procedures, that person may be assigned to document procedural changes.

♦ Identify which tasks in the implementation plan are deadlines and/or milestones.

♦ Identify resources needed to implement changes. For example, if new equipment must be purchased, how much will it cost, what vendor will be used, when does it need to be installed, etc.

The implementation plan is the road map to ensuring portions of the redesigned process are not overlooked. The more time and detailed information included in your implementation plan, the easier the implementation will progress. Just as with any type of business venture, the more planning done up front, the easier the follow-up work will be. Once a detailed implementation plan is developed, the initial team can review the tasks and determine which team members should be assigned to various tasks.

Team Member Roles

After tasks are identified and detailed in the implementation plan, people with specific skill sets should be assigned to roles or specific tasks they are responsible for completing. For instance, the redesigned system may consist of consolidating several departments and implementing appropriate technology to facilitate this change. In this scenario, certain team members will be assigned to address the technical issues of installing and configuring the required technology which may consist of electronic mail, groupware applications, or client/server technologies. Another member may be assigned the role of facilitating change at the departmental management level. Both of these functions are extremely important to the success of the project; however, they require two very different skill sets. It is important to identify the strengths of each team member and assign roles in the implementation project accordingly. The project's technical guru should not be assigned to work at assisting management in accepting the changes and the human resource specialist, who is empathetic to how change affects people, should not be assigned to head up the technical implementation portion of the project.

A matrix is a useful technique to relate team members and their associated skills to the tasks required by the implementation plan (see Figure 8.4). Data flow diagramming and matrices are also valuable techniques that can be used in many different contexts (see Appendix A). If outside consultants will be used during the implementation phase, internal team members who will work with them and learn from them should be identified at this time.

Deadlines and Milestones

During the planning task it is important to identify deadlines and milestones and to allocate specific amounts of time for each task of the implementation plan. Typically a task will expand to fill the time allotted for it. In other words, without deadlines, the project can go on indefinitely. It is human nature to want to produce the best possible product (if you subscribe to Theory Y motivational axiom), and if deadlines are not set, the work will be fine-tuned longer than necessary. Of course, the deadlines should be realistic. People work best under some pressure, but that pressure should not be constant or overwhelming. Building deadlines into the project ensures that the project moves forward on schedule. When milestones are reached, such as the detailed plan is complete, the team should celebrate the success. It is just as important to celebrate successfully met deadlines or reached milestones in the project as it is to keep the project on track. Time lines are important, but team-building and morale maintenance are equally important aspects of managing the project.

Team Member	Write Programs	Document Policy Changes	Conduct Town Hall Meetings	Schedule Training Sessions	Purchase Equipment	Conduct Training	... add'l. tasks
Candy		X		X		X	
Constance	X		X		X		
David	X				X		
Deborah	X	X		X			
Kathy				X		X	
Maria	X				X		
Milan	X				X		
Rich				X	X	X	
Samantha		X	X				
...add'l team members							

Figure 8.4 A matrix is simply a two-dimensional, tabular representation of the relationship between two things. In this example, the matrix is used to depict the relationship between team members' skill sets and the tasks required during implementation of a redesigned process.

Resources

The resources needed to successfully implement the redesigned changes should be identified as explicitly as possible. If any portion of the implementation will be outsourced, it should be identified at this time. Also, if training is required for the technical staff to implement the technology changes recommended, then this must be identified. For example, when organizations move from mainframe systems to client/server LAN-based environments, additional training for the technical staff will be required. If any hardware or software must be purchased, this is the time to stipulate the cost as well as the vendor. The resources require specific identification now because orders must be placed and delivery times must be calculated into the implementation time line. Initial equipment estimates were provided to senior management during the planning phase of the project, and more detailed estimates were forwarded during the redesign and transition phases. The moneys should already be earmarked for the project; however, the paperwork and any unfinished negotiations need to occur at this time. After the plan is completed, detailed tasks are specified, personnel and corporate culture issues are incorporated into the tasks, team members are identified, deadlines assigned, and resources requested. Now it is time to implement the redesigned processes.

Manual and Automated Process Implementation

Manual Processes

In most BPR processes manual portions of the project will be divided from automated portions. The manual portion deals with the organization changes that may occur, the job responsibilities that will change, and the policies and procedures which will be altered. The implementation of the manual processes can be completed simultaneously with the automated processes. Different team members will work on each manual or automated portion. Constant communication must exist between the team subsets (manual procedure changes, change facilitation, and technical implementation). However, these tasks can occur simultaneously for the most part. There will be some overlap, since no system exists without affecting other systems. Changes in manual procedures will affect portions of the automated system and vice versa. However, if constant communication exists, the manual and automated portions can be developed simultaneously with any issues affecting both addressed by both teams.

Human factors are a part of the manual process changes that will affect both the manual and automated portions of the redesigned process. The automated portion of the project deals mainly with installing hardware and software, programming, or integrating systems. Usually the team members on the technical subteam are capable technicians, but may be unable to deal with the personnel issues involved in facilitating change. Based upon their skill set, focus groups who discuss how changes will affect departments and other such tasks are better led by individuals who will be working with changing the manual portions of the redesigned processes.

Policies, as well as procedures, may require change. Organizational structures may also change. These are difficult issues, but must be addressed directly and immediately. The longer information is withheld from staff, the more suspicious they will be of any changes announced to them. How policies and procedures are changed directly relates to the culture of the organization and how successful the implementation will be. Whatever the decision to handle changing policies may be, communication should be open and flow freely both up and down the organizational hierarchy. As organizations downsize and reduce the levels of middle management, the need for communication increases in order to keep everyone informed and working toward the same goals.

Automated Processes

The part of implementation that addresses the automated portions of the redesigned process is typically thought of as implementation in the system development life cycle. Many of the commercial methodologies such as STRADIS provide detailed guidelines for implementation plans of automated systems. The main point to remember is that the automated system is only a portion of the BPR project. Thus, it is only a portion of the implementation phase. Facilitating the change, introducing it in such a manner that people are willing to change is a vital portion of any BPR implementation.

Systems Development

If an organization follows any type of guidelines for implementing computer systems, those steps could be folded into the BPR project for this portion of the implementation plan. Many technical issues are involved in implementing new technologies. Systems and other types of testing, data conversion issues, and throughput are just some of the concerns addressed during implementing the automated portion of the BPR project. If an organization has an internal IS staff, they should have guidelines for developing and implementing computer systems. These guidelines can be incorporated into the BPR implementation plan for the automated portion of the implementation. Consultants can also provide implementation guidelines for computer systems. Whatever the guidelines adopted, they must be incorporated into a larger implementation plan that addresses the manual processes being changed as well as facilitate the change itself. Figure 7.6 illustrates where traditional computer systems development methodologies and guidelines can be incorporated into the BPR project.

Documentation

Whatever the methodology chosen for implementing the automated portion of the BPR project, documentation is critical. Manual processes must be documented as well. However, if the automated portion is not documented, there is no way to recreate the logic of the system if the programmers or systems developers leave the organization. If you hire outside contract programmers or consultants to develop the automated system, proper documentation must be received. If internal IS personnel work on the project, then the same documentation standards should be maintained. Documentation should include data flow diagrams and entity-relationship diagrams. If these modeling techniques are used by the redesign team, and enhanced by the transition team, the implementation team will need only to adjust them to show the level of detail required for documentation purposes. This is the benefit of using a standard modeling technique throughout the entire BPR project.

Testing

Testing the automated systems, obtaining feedback from personnel on the manual procedures, and ensuring that both work together effectively are required before the redesigned system is used and people are trained. Prior to testing an automated system, a testing plan must be established. Testing plans used within current IS operations will probably suffice. However, if testing plans are not standardized or non-existent, then time should be spent to develop testing plans for all automated systems development. Several types of tests should be initiated and staff should be consulted before implementing any changes. A focus group or other type of discussion group would be helpful for this purpose.

Training

Training encompasses many considerations. Change facilitation is a combination of training, focus groups, and town hall discussions. End-user training for the automated portions of the redesigned process must also be considered. However, beyond teaching people how to use the new automated system, the training should include a more in-depth knowledge transfer of what will be accomplished. If training can include why the processes were changed and why the solutions decided upon were accepted, the staff will have a better opportunity to react if conditions change. If the redesigned process remains static, no long-term benefit is obtained by the organization. To achieve long-term benefits, the staff must be trained to use the redesigned processes, both manual and automated, and be informed as to why the changes were made in the first place. In this way, they can facilitate future enhancements to the redesigned process and continually improve it. BPR should not be a final solution, but rather the beginning of a continuous improvement effort. The training aspect of the BPR implementation plan should convey this information to staff and management.

ASSESSMENT

Provisions for assessment should be part of the implementation plan. The redesigned process should be assessed, after an appropriate period of usage has occurred, in order to determine if the redesigned changes met the initial objectives identified at the beginning of the project. *Causal analysis*— basically, the act of determining what caused a specific situation to occur—should be completed. In this context, the redesigned process should be assessed to determine if it met the initial goals. If it did not, it should be determined why it didn't. If that next step, to *determine why the redesigned process failed to meet the goals stipulated at the beginning of the project* is not completed, the next BPR project may also miss its mark. Understanding and analyzing failure is much more productive than studying success. By analyzing what went wrong and why, and learning from those mistakes, the same pitfalls in future BPR projects can be avoided.

The other type of assessment that needs to be addressed is how this redesigned process can exist without becoming archaic and outdated like the preceding process it replaced. In other words, how can the redesigned process continually improve? On-going assessment and evaluation must be built-in to the redesigned process itself. For instance, control over certain aspects of the redesigned process can be distributed to those employees involved in that aspect of the process. This is the empowerment concept, which has been espoused in management journals and texts over the past years. However, if true empowerment is built-in to redesigned processes, they will not become obsolete. The process will become dynamic, changing as the needs of the organization change. This is the ultimate goal of business process redesign.

CHAPTER HIGHLIGHTS

✎ Implementation is the part of the project when all the previously developed plans and redesign concepts must come together. This can be the most challenging part of the entire process.

✎ Technical skills are necessary during implementation because the majority of process redesign projects implement some form of technology to facilitate change within the organization. There is, however, a need for change management and facilitation skills. Because of the need for such a diversified skill set, the implementation team is actually the conglomeration of three subteams, each with a special focus.

Change Facilitation
Technology Implementation
Manual Procedure Changes

✎ Several issues affect implementation including the environment and management's perception of the employee. An environment where risk-taking and participative management are employed will provide a fertile ground for business process redesign to take hold.

✎ The shrinking ranks of middle management is a trend that affects business reengineering. Since technologies are changing the role of middle management, and in many cases eliminating it, it is important to take this into account when introducing change.

♦ Middle management is no longer needed to disseminate information throughout the organization. Electronic mail, bulletin boards, and various other technologies are replacing this need within the company.

♦ Middle management is no longer needed to gather and summarize information. Database systems and executive query tools provide the infrastructure necessary for this type of function to be completed.

Advocates from all levels of management are necessary in order to facilitate the changes proposed by the redesign effort; understanding the changing, and sometimes eroding, role of middle management is imperative to successful implementation.

✎ Turn a negative aspect into a positive one in order to successfully facilitate change. Identifying possible problems or challenges before implementation begins is vital. Once the negative aspects of a project implementation are identified, steps can be taken to either minimize those aspects or turn them into a positive attribute to help facilitate the proposed changes.

✎ The corporate culture within the organization is a conglomeration of management's values and morals. The corporate culture can facilitate or hinder change. Whichever type of culture exists in the organization, the first step is to identify it and determine a strategy to implement change.

✎ Planning is still the first item that needs to be addressed. There are many different tasks being accomplished simultaneously; therefore, several subteams will be necessary to address change facilitation, manual procedure changes, and technical implementation. Both manual and automated processes need to be addressed during implementation. Team members with the appropriate skills need to be identified and assigned to subteams.

✎ Coordination of the implementation phase is critical in order to assure success. Facilitating change is a key role that must be accomplished during this phase. Personnel, as well as corporate culture issues will affect the success of the project. The team should be aware of these issues and plan accordingly.

✎ Change is difficult, and without planning and coordination, inertia will take over. Understanding the human tendency to prefer status quo is important to planning for the changes. The facilitation subteam will deal mostly with these types of issues.

✎ Documentation, testing, training, and priorities issues must be addressed during the implementation phase of the project. Without a solid, well-defined implementation, the redesigned process will not succeed.

✎ Assessment is a necessary final step to the redesign process. In order to determine whether the changes to the process were successful, they must be assessed. Chapter 9 provides a detailed discussion of assessment issues.

PART III

Recap/Final Thoughts

There Is No Silver Bullet

THE BPR PROCESS

The phases and tasks provided in this book represent an outlined methodology for implementing organizational reengineering concepts. The main emphasis has been placed on BPR projects because it is recommended that you attempt several BPR projects before an enterprise-wide business reengineering project is attempted (see Figure 9.1). There are four major types of reengineering projects which can be pursued:

♦ Technology application
♦ Work-flow analysis
♦ Business process redesign
♦ Enterprise-wide business reengineering

The type of project depends on the scope of the project. Most times, when the term reengineering is used, the broadest scope is assumed—enterprise-wide business reengineering. However, many organizations have undertaken work-flow analysis or technology application and identified the projects as reengineering. The differences between these reengineering projects can be compared to the differences

---

Business Reengineering Guidelines

BPR Phases	*Tasks within phases*
Planning	Senior Management Commitment
	Determine Priorities
	◆ Organizational goals
	◆ Strategic plan
	Identify Scope
	Determine Initial Feasibility
	◆ Technical
	◆ Economical
	◆ Political
	Determine Potential Benefit
	Identify Core Team Members
Redesign	Tactical Planning for Redesign Phase
	◆ Identify additional team members
	Determine Scope
	◆ Analyze problem or opportunity
	◆ Customer emphasis
	Evaluate Feasibility in More Detail
	◆ Technical feasibility
	◆ Economical feasibility
	◆ Political feasibility
	Requirements Definition
	◆ What current process/system does
	Redesign Process
	◆ What new process/system should do
	◆ Brainstorming
	Redesign Recommendation
	Tactical Planning for Transition Phase
	Identify Key Transition Team Members

(continued on next page)

BPR Phases	*Tasks within phases*
Transition	Determine Alternatives
	♦ Strategic analysis
	♦ Strategic design
	Evaluate Alternatives
	♦ Evaluate solutions against requirements
	Tactical Study
	♦ Solutions proposal
	Tactical Planning for Implementation Phase
Implementation	Develop an Understanding of Issues Affecting Implementation
	Refine Implementation Plan
	♦ Identify specific tasks to be accomplished
	♦ Identify team member roles
	♦ Determine deadlines and milestones
	♦ Determine resources required
	♦ Differential manual and automated processes
	Develop Testing Plan
	Develop Training Plan
	Implement Manual and Automated Portions Concurrently
	Test Automated Portions
	Train Staff
	Assess Implemented Redesigned Process

Figure 9.1 The planning tasks outlined here provide a guideline for undertaking business reengineering projects regardless of the scope (enterprise-wide reengineering project, BPR projects, work-flow analysis projects or technology application projects). The phases and tasks outlined here constitute a methodology for business reengineering, specifically BPR as discussed in this book, which can be tailored to the needs of each organization. In order for this methodology to be effective it must be customized, detailed tasks identified, and it must be continually improved. This information provides the guidelines or starting point.

between different types of total quality management (TQM) initiatives. Some organizations incorporate redesigning business processes within the TQM projects, while others view TQM as simply improving customer service using existing processes.

In order for any organization to dynamically change its environment, all types of reengineering should be undertaken at different levels. Global, cross-functional teams should be working on enterprise-wide business reengineering projects and business process redesign projects while department heads can simultaneously implement work-flow analysis and technology application. Figure 9.2 illustrates the type of reengineering project as it relates to the level of involvement by management. Technology application and work-flow analysis projects can be accomplished within a specific department and several projects can occur simultaneously. Coordination of these efforts must, however, be maintained to be sure that duplication of effort does not occur. A quality committee or some other type of oversight group could coordinate the various intradepartmental projects occurring within the organization. BPR and enterprise-wide business reengineering projects can occur with a greater level of senior management involvement. A dynamic organization that is able to succeed into the next century will have several types of reengineering projects and total quality control initiatives underway. Coordination of these efforts is vital, since no system or process exists within a vacuum.

Technology Application

Technology Application focuses on one process usually within one department. It usually does not radically change any existing procedures, but merely automates existing processes. One example of this type of reengineering project replaces manual forms within an organization with an electronic forms package without eliminating or consolidating forms or examining underlying business purposes for the manual forms. Simply automating or applying technology to preexisting processes will not provide any breakthrough

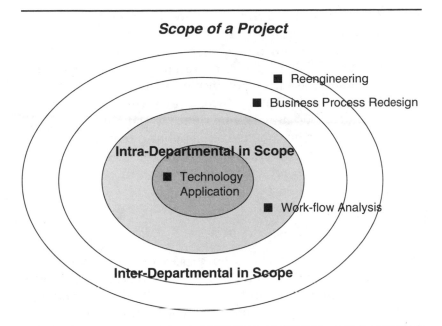

Figure 9.2 The scope of a project can be viewed as narrow to all-encompassing. Technology application projects have the narrowest scope as compared to reengineering projects which span the entire organization or a major portion of it. The scope of a project increases as more processes, people, and information are included in the project. Technology application and work-flow analysis projects usually involve only one department. If they cross departments, only a few departments will be involved. BPR and reengineering projects span many departments. In the case of reengineering projects, every department may be involved.

changes. However, it may free staff time in order to allow them to maintain their current level of service while working on larger reengineering projects.

Care must be taken, however, to ensure that other processes affected by applying technology are changed accordingly. At this level of reengineering, the reliance upon other systems and processes within the organization is strong. If changes to one system occur, through applying technology, analysis must be done and appropriate changes made to the various processes that interface with the redesigned process. When the focus of the reengineering project is narrow, such as in the case of applying technology, only a limited number of processes will be changed; however, it will interact with a great deal of other processes. Those interfaces need to be addressed. For example, if the billing system is automated, how inventory, accounts receivable, accounts payable, and other subsystems relate to the automated billing process must be considered. Applying technology without appropriately adjusting the manual or other automated processes that interact with that system, will prove counterproductive.

Work-flow Analysis

Work-flow analysis focuses on processes either within or between departments. The scope of a work-flow analysis project is larger than that of simply applying technology, although technology may change. It includes altering or redesigning processes within or between departments. Departmental procedures may change; however, corporate policies or organizational restructuring would be beyond the scope of work-flow analysis. Changes made as a result of a work-flow analysis project tend to be incremental. In other words, changes are built upon the existing processes. The way things are done is fine-tuned rather than altered. Because the scope is smaller than a BPR or reengineering project, the time to complete the project is also less. Work-flow analysis projects can be viewed as technology applications which may automate more than one process. The scope of the project is expanded from simply applying technology to a specific process; however, many manual or automated systems that interface with the redesigned work-flow process need to be addressed.

Business Process Redesign

Business process redesign focuses on the underlying business reasons for certain processes under consideration. This text concentrates primarily on BPR-type reengineering projects, basically, because the scope of a BPR project is large enough to allow major changes to occur, yet small enough to be manageable. It is desirable to try to redesign a manageable process and understand the human factors associated with implementing a specific change before redesigning the way things are done through a reengineering project. Usually the scope of a BPR project includes the following: automated systems (especially legacy systems), manual processes, organizational structure and reporting structures, as well as corporate policies. BPR usually involves critically analyzing major processes within the organization that affect multiple departments. The major obstacle to any reengineering effort is addressing the issue of change.

Technically, almost any type of process can be redesigned to be more effective and efficient. For instance, technology exists today that can allow corporate employees to work at home. A major obstacle to this paradigm shift—working at home rather than in the office—is not technical. The major hurdle to overcome is management's need to physically oversee employees. The current assumption is if management can see the individual at a desk, then the employee is working. This is probably not a valid assumption, since a person can be at a desk and not be working, or working when away from the desk. However, in order for working at home to be a viable option, better and clearer goals need to be articulated by management. Also assessment of the employee's ability to attain those goals needs to be identified. Therefore, the obstacle to working at home is not technical, but related to management's need to change their concept of what work is and how it is assessed. This is a major change from current business thinking, and is the type of issue that is addressed within the scope of a BPR project.

Enterprise-wide Business Reengineering

Enterprise-wide business reengineering focuses on the underlying vision of the organization. Drastically changing the organizational structure, eliminating departments and middle management, outsourcing entire functions, and realigning corporate goals with current products or services produced are issues addressed at this level of reengineering. Ultimately, reengineering the business provides the most opportunity for improvement. However, it is also the most difficult to accomplish without any prior experience. Reengineering, defined in this context as all-encompassing, is very rarely successful the first time. Just as you need to walk before you run, it is useful to understand all of the political, social, and technical aspects of reengineering before a major overhaul of the organization is attempted. BPR projects, with their reduced scope, provide staff with the required experience to move on to reengineering, producing radical changes within the scope of the entire organization.

There Is No Quick Fix

The methodology outlined in this book utilizes existing systems development expertise available in most organizations during the transition and implementation phases of the project. By combining traditional systems development methodologies based on the SDLC into the broader scope of a BPR project, information gathered in the redesign phase can be shared with individuals in the transition phase. If the same techniques, such as data flow diagramming and entity-relationship diagramming as discussed in Appendix A are used, resources need not be expended to gather that information. Of course, each organization needs to customize tasks in order to take advantage of specific personnel and organizational requirements.

There is no quick fix. There is no silver bullet.

Reengineering existing business processes is a time-consuming and arduous task. But the potential benefits are enormous.

Reengineering business processes is not only time-consuming, but also continually evolving. Reengineering cannot be done once and forgotten. It is not something that stands on its own. Reengineering incorporates years of management theory and concepts such as management by objective, total quality management, continuous quality improvement, employee empowerment, paradigm shift, and visioning. If reengineering is viewed as another management fad, it will not be successful. Reengineering embodies much of the management principals and theories espoused over the last decades. Critically looking at business processes and functions, and continually assessing ways to improve the business is what management concepts and theories have promised. All of these concepts are built on sound principal; however, they must be incorporated into the culture of the organization to be effective. Reengineering alone will not provide the sought-after benefits of reduced costs and increased quality. However, reengineering coupled with employee empowerment, focused on continually improving processes toward an ultimate corporate vision will provide an atmosphere suitable for growth and adaptation. Adaptation is the key to survival for organizations today and in the twenty-first century.

If time and effort are spent to redesign a process which becomes static, the company remains in the same predicament; the process will eventually be obsolete. In effect, today's redesigned process will become tomorrow's obsolete legacy system. In order to ensure that this does not happen, continuous improvement elements should be built-in to the redesigned system. Overall, reengineering must be combined with sound management theory and practice in order to succeed. If processes are redesigned, yet employees are not empowered to adjust certain parameters within their control, the redesigned process will become stagnant.

Meta Process Concept

The term *meta process* denotes information accumulated or maintained concerning the process of redesigning processes. It is similar to the computing term meta data, which denotes information or data maintained about database elements. Maintaining information about the process used to redesign other processes can be a confusing concept. However, just as it is important to evaluate changes made to a specific process which was redesigned, it is important to document and improve the steps used to redesign those processes. The SEI model adapted earlier illustrated that once a BPR project was completed, it could be documented in such a way to make it repeatable. That documentation is considered meta process information. Meta process information can contain answers to the following questions:

♦ How long did the BPR project take? How much time was estimated at the beginning of the project? Were the various phases completed according to the initial time line?

♦ What resources were initially identified and which of those resources were actually used?

♦ What types of problems were encountered when trying to introduce change to the organization? How were those problems addressed?

♦ What types of ideas were generated from the redesign phase? Were the ideas innovative? How could the process be improved to generate more creative redesign ideas?

♦ Was the transformation between redesign and transition phase, as well as the transition and implementation phase smooth?

♦ Were models developed in one phase useful in other phases?

Meta process information provides the necessary data to analyze the tasks or steps involved in redesigning business processes. A distinction between outcome versus process should be understood. The outcome of a reengineering project is a redesigned business process—changes to the organization occur. Reengineering is also a process in and of itself. There are tasks that need to be completed in order to redesign business processes. It is important to improve the tasks or methodology used to redesign business processes. Meta process data provides documentation to assist with that endeavor. Meta process data should be maintained in some form, whether in paper form organized in a binder, or an electronic compound document. In any case, the information should be readily accessible to future BPR teams in order to provide them with knowledge they would otherwise have to experience themselves. The purpose of maintaining meta process information is to eliminate the need to "reinvent the wheel" every time a BPR project is undertaken. In order to improve reengineering efforts, understanding of past mistakes and successes is necessary.

CONTINUOUS IMPROVEMENT

Continuous improvement is a total quality management concept that addresses the issues of continually measuring and assessing the quality of a given product, service, or process. Many companies have named their quality improvement programs with acronyms such as CQI (continuous quality improvement) to denote the importance of continually monitoring and assessing quality. In fact many TQM programs incorporate various types of business process redesign. The quality management concept is important to business process redesign because any new processes or systems that are implemented within an organization should be continually monitored. If you change the way you do business, and do not assess this change, how can you determine if your efforts were successful? Continuous improvement applies in two ways to business process redesign projects: the redesign process itself, and the outcome of the redesign project—the newly redesigned business process (see Figure 9.3).

Continually Improving Outcome

The newly redesigned business process should have built-in measurement and evaluation capability that determines redesign success and allows for new changes. Without continuous improvement built-in to the new designed business process, any long-term benefits cannot be achieved because the environment is continually changing—current processes have become outdated. This ability to measure project outcomes should be ongoing in order to ensure that changes in

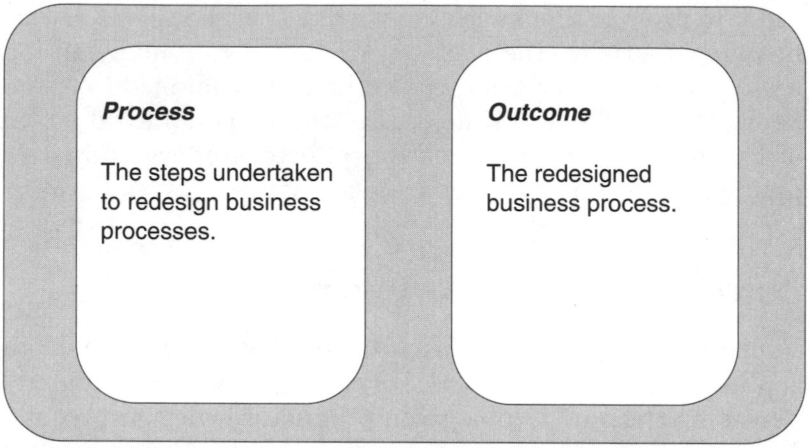

Process

The steps undertaken
to redesign business
processes.

Outcome

The redesigned
business process.

Continuous improvement relates to BPR projects on two levels. First,
continually monitor the steps in the BPR methodology and fine-tune them to
meet the needs of the organization. Second, build quantifiable assessment
into the redesigned processes recommended by the BPR team. For example, if the BPR team addressed the billing process within an organization;
quantifiable measurement must be built-in to the redesigned billing process
in order to ascertain if the changes were beneficial to the organization.

Outcome versus Process

	Examples of improving process	Examples of improving outcome
Paying Monthly Bills	Automate check printing	Verify checks sent
Produce Widgets	Adjust assembly line	Inspect and discard faulty widgets

The quality of the outcome is directly related to the quality of the process.
Outcome cannot be improved without improving the process used to
generate the outcome. The quality of widgets cannot be improved by
simply inspecting and discarding faulty widgets. However, by adjusting the
process which produces the widgets, improvement can be obtained.

Figure 9.3 Facets of continuous improvement for BPR.

the environment are recognized and appropriate modifications to the newly redesigned business process are initiated.

The business process redesign project should have measurements built-in to it so that evaluations of the redesigned process as well as possible improvements can be incorporated. The question, "How do you know that the effort has been successful?" must be asked.

In order to determine the success of a business process redesign project, the purpose of the project must be clear and measurable. If the purpose of a redesign project is to improve customer service, how will the success of the project be measured? Unless the goal "improve customer service" is quantifiably defined, it will be impossible to develop accurate measurements of success. Therefore, at the beginning of a business process redesign project, the goal or desired outcome should be clearly defined. If this is not initially done, determining measurement and building assessment into the redesigned process will be futile. In other words, clearly define what the purpose of the redesign project is before you try to determine how you will measure whether it was successful.

After a quantifiable objective is determined at the beginning of the BPR project, continuous improvement elements should be built-in to the project during all of the phases. Throughout the entire redesign project (redesign, transition, and implementation), continuous improvement should be considered.

In the redesign phase of the project, continuous improvement should be incorporated into the recommended redesign project—not as a separate issue, but as an integral part of the redesigned process.

♦ During the planning phase, the issue of continuous improvement and assessment should be discussed and prioritized within the overall scope of the project.
♦ During the transition phase, continuous improvement should be factored into how the redesigned process will be implemented. If feedback is to be obtained at specific intervals of time, it should be documented in the redesigned process at this point.

♦ During the implementation phase, continuous improvement will be incorporated into the newly redesigned processes.

Assessment of the tasks accomplished during the redesign project (process) is done at the end of the implementation phase; however, the assessment of the redesigned process (outcome) cannot be completed immediately. The redesigned process must become part of the organization's procedures for an agreed-to time period before it can be evaluated. In essence, continuous improvement should be at the core of the redesigned process, and not addressed as a separate issue in order to be effective.

To reiterate, business process redesign is not a one-time exercise that can be completed and forgotten.

♦ Once a new process is implemented within an organization, ongoing assessment should also be implemented.
♦ Changes in the environment may make the newly redesigned process obsolete in the future—such changes as new competition, new government regulations, and technological advances.

Organizations today have many problems because procedures and processes were put into place years ago and never re-evaluated. Every organization contains instances of obsolete procedures or policies that are still adhered to because "that's the way it's always been done." In order to ensure that any changes in processes and procedures introduced today do not become tomorrow's nuisances, continuous assessment and improvement of the processes must be built-in to the new system.

Building Continuous Improvement into the Redesign Process

One way that continuous improvement can be built-in to redesigned business processes is to have six-month or annual reviews of the process itself. These reviews check that the goals of the initial project have been met. If goals have not been met, or only minimally increased from the original processes, then the system should be analyzed again. Just as the initial goals of the redesign project must be quantified, so too must the measurement criteria. Before the system can be measured, however, measurement methods must be created. The idea of re-evaluating the project outcome at specified time intervals is imperative to the long-term success of the organization, especially because changes in the environment occur more rapidly with every year. It is estimated today that a college student's technical expertise becomes obsolete within three years. This means that the technology learned as a freshman is obsolete before graduation. The same change acceleration holds true in the business environment. Therefore, if current or redesigned processes are not re-evaluated every couple of years, they may become obsolete, allowing the competition an edge.

Another way to continuously improve the redesigned process (outcome) is to design it with flexibility in mind. If the redesigned process is designed in such a way that changes can be made to the process as they occur, then the odds that the process will remain a vital and effective part of the organization is increased. If processes or procedures are put in place which require executive signature authority for even minor changes to occur, chances are the process will become stagnant. However, if the concept of employee empowerment is built into the redesigned process, the opportunity for change and adaptation is increased. If employees are able to alter certain aspects of the redesigned process within their control, they are more likely to take ownership of the process and continually assess and improve it. Thought must be given not only to initially implementing the redesigned process, but also to how the redesigned process will adapt and grow with changes in the environment occurring ever more rapidly.

Continually Improving the Process

Continuous process improvements apply to the methods or steps an organization incorporates into the redesign. Chapters 5 through 8 provide guidelines for implementing a business process redesign project. However, since every organization is unique, these guidelines should be adapted to different circumstances.

♦ Once the steps or guidelines which meet the needs of your organization are identified, they should be assessed.
♦ The steps or guidelines used should not become absolute.
♦ Continually look at how you redesign your processes (the process of redesigning processes) and make modifications to the steps as appropriate.
♦ In order to improve the outcome quality, the process itself must be effective.

A business process redesign project is actually a process in itself. A process is defined by Funk and Wagnalls as "a course or method of operations in the production of something." The outcome of a business process redesign project is a newly redesigned business process or system, just as the outcome of a manufacturing process is a product. Both business process redesign projects and manufacturing processes have outcomes or products. It is sometimes easier to see an outcome of a manufacturing process because it is tangible. However, the outcome of a business process redesign project is a new system or process, set of procedures, policies, and automated systems. The only tangible proof of the entire effort you can see are system models, such as data-flow diagrams, similar in concept to the blueprints used for building a house. Even using the analogy of the blueprints—the house is eventually built and a physical manifestation of the planning work previously done can be seen. With a business process redesign project, there never is a physical manifestation of the work completed. The system or newly designed process cannot be seen, except by new steps or procedures employees complete differently. The newly designed process cannot be felt. The computers, forms, and so on used are physical representations of the system; however, you cannot touch them. Because redesigned processes are abstract, it is sometimes difficult to view them as an outcome or product.

In order to assure the success of business process redesign efforts, the redesign or reengineering process must be continually assessed and improved. Just as improvement to a product cannot be made unless adjustments to the assembly line are made, the quality of the redesigned business processes (outcomes of BPR efforts) cannot be improved without changing the steps or methods used. If an organization undertakes a BPR project and it is not successful, future projects will not be successful without changing the steps which developed the initial BPR project. This concept is analogous to a golfer who continually drives his ball into a sand trap. Changing the ball will not change the outcome! Without changing the process (the swing itself) the outcome (the ball landing in the sand trap) will not change. One reason that many organizations are having trouble solving problems related to existing processes and systems is not their inability to recognize the problem. In many cases, the problem lies in outmoded methods for problem identification and solution. In other words, they are using an inappropriate golf swing for the specific situation. The processes or methodologies used to solve problems are obsolete. Therefore, the outcomes or solutions arrived at are not optimum.

Implementing Continuous Improvement

The importance of continually assessing the steps or methodology (the process) used to redesign business processes as well as the redesigned processes themselves (the outcome) have been discussed in the preceding sections of this chapter. How to apply continuous improvement to a business process redesign effort requires two levels of continuous improvement.

♦ First, improving the redesign effort itself should be addressed. The steps or methodology used to redesign the business processes should be monitored and fine-tuned. The guidelines provided in this text should be used as a starting point. Assess the steps used to redesign a given business process. This assessment should take place at the end of every business process redesign project.

♦ Secondly, the outcome of the redesign project, or the new
system and procedures put into place within an organization, should be re-evaluated to determine if goals have
been achieved. Since the outcome is a process (redesigned
business process), continuous improvement should be
designed into the redesigned process itself.

MANAGING CHANGE

Even though change management is mentioned when discussion about implementing change occurs, *change cannot
be managed*—not in the true sense of management. Change
cannot be controlled, nor should it be. Of course, an organization does not want random change occurring without some
type of strategic plan or goals in place. However, the environment must be conducive to change. Specific projects
which implement change can be managed using project management techniques and tools; however, the change itself
can only thrive in a dynamic organization.

Leadership versus Management

Reengineering the entire business or portions of the business (business process redesign) requires strong leadership
from senior management. *Leaders*, rather than *managers*
are required to initiate change within the organization.
Much more than semantics is involved when discussing leadership versus management. Leaders provide an environment in which change is dynamic. Change should not be
initiated for change's sake; however, a static environment is
not healthy for the organization or its employees. Executives and key employees' inability to *lead* poses a problem in
many organizations today. To manage an operation or process involves control, working with predictability, and eliminating or minimizing change. Leadership can be summed
up as improving processes and business while management
is involved in maintaining status quo. In order for any redesign efforts to be effective, senior staff must possess leader-

ship skills. Major changes in the organization require a champion, someone who continually raises issues and is willing to commit resources.

Organizational Culture

The culture of an organization must be open to change. In order to establish an environment in which business process redesign can occur at all levels within the organization, everyone must feel comfortable with change and taking risk. As explained in earlier chapters, business process redesign can occur at the interdepartmental level with cross-functional teams working on changing major processes in the organization. The organizational culture must support a team environment. Major changes will not occur without multiple individuals working on the project and buying into the proposed changes. It is difficult for many individuals to work in teams. In western society, the educational system, from kindergarten through post-secondary, frowns upon "sharing" information. Because of this educational background, working as part of a team is difficult. Many colleges and universities are currently building team participation into their curriculums to overcome this trend. However, the concept of teams is contrary to American culture where individualism is revered. In order for reengineering to be successful, an organization must provide an environment where individualism can be accepted, while simultaneously encouraging team work.

While major, interdepartmental projects are being carried out, on a smaller scale, work-flow analysis and technology application projects can occur within departments. Not all change needs to be major or radical to benefit the organization. A myriad of small, incremental improvements to processes can have an astounding effect. Both levels of change, interdepartmental and smaller scope, must exist in order for the organization to be truly dynamic and in a position to take advantage of changing external conditions in the environment such as governmental regulations, international trade regulations, and competition.

Organizational Planning

Leaders within the organization must champion redesigning processes—change. The organizational climate or culture must be conducive to change. But change without direction is chaos. The organization must foster change which synchronizes with its mission. Everyone within the organization must share a vision against which changes and redesign process projects can be evaluated. A strategic plan must be developed and embraced by all levels of management, as well as by staff (see Figure 9.4). In order for an organization to be truly effective, everyone in that organization must know the direction they should be working toward.

A vision is useless if it is not shared. It must be communicated with the staff. In this way proposed redesign projects can be evaluated against that mission to determine whether the effort should be undertaken. Figure 9.5 illustrates the various categories a BPR project can fall into. A strategic plan has

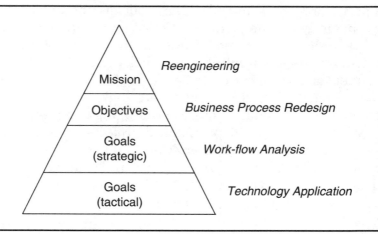

Figure 9.4   Reengineering projects can be classified based on project. The type of reengineering project can also be classified according to its relationship with corporate planning. The mission statement describes the basic business an organization is in, as well as its underlying philosophy and vision. Reengineering projects address this mission statement because they tackle the question "what business are we in?"

Business Reengineering Project Categories

High Risk for failure High Payback	Low Risk for failure High Payback
High Risk for failure Low Payback	Low Risk for failure Low Payback

Figure 9.5   Business reengineering or BPR projects in particular can fall into four categories. This matrix shows the combination of possibilities using risk and payback as the two factors evaluated. All BPR projects must be in line with the corporate goals; however, any projects undertaken must also provide an opportunity for substantial benefits while allowing ample opportunity for success. The ideal situation is a project which has a low risk for failure while providing substantial benefits (see shaded area).

many components; the highest-level or most abstract is the mission statement. The *mission statement* should provide documentation of the organization's vision. It is difficult to tie any specific BPR project or work-flow analysis project into the corporate mission. Reengineering projects would address this level of the strategic plan, defining the basic business an organization is in and its vision for the future. Reengineering questions addressed at this level of planning include:

◆   What business have we been in?
◆   What business should we be in the future and why?
◆   Who is our primary customer? (An organization, through a reengineering effort may determine that retail rather than wholesale, or vice versa, is an appropriate redirection of the business.)

The *objectives* of an organization are derived from the mission statement. The objectives of an organization are statements which support the mission or overall direction of the organization by identifying long-term, nonquantifiable direction. BPR projects would provide solutions to objectives identified by an organization. Objectives help determine which business processes should be analyzed and which must be supported by the organization. The objective provides the problem or opportunity which a BPR project would address. For example, one objective might be to increase the international market share in at least three free market economies. A business process redesign project utilizing the guidelines provided in this book would then examine innovative ways in order to accomplish this by rethinking the way current processes are done.

After objectives supporting the organization's mission

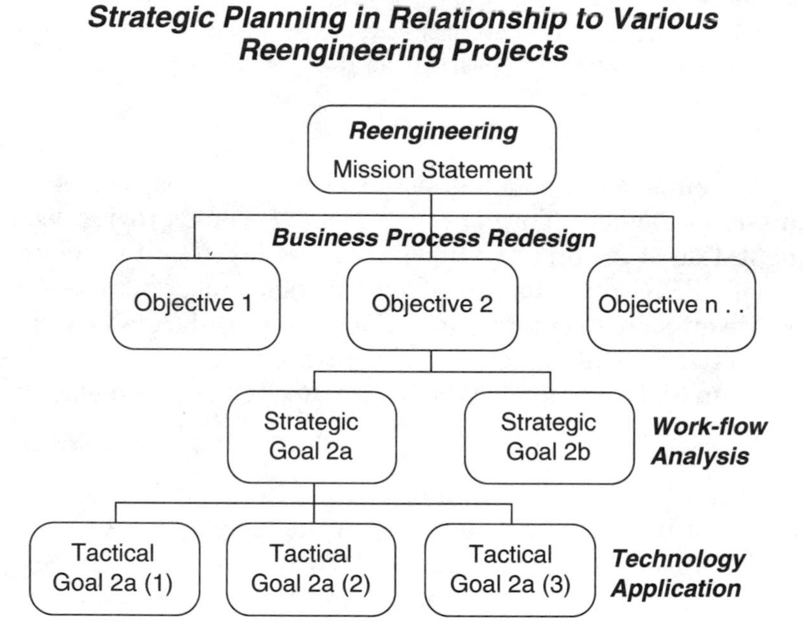

Strategic Planning in Relationship to Various Reengineering Projects

Reengineering
Mission Statement

Business Process Redesign

Objective 1   Objective 2   Objective n . .

Strategic Goal 2a   Strategic Goal 2b   **Work-flow Analysis**

Tactical Goal 2a (1)   Tactical Goal 2a (2)   Tactical Goal 2a (3)   **Technology Application**

Figure 9.6 This diagram illustrates the relationship of the corporate mission statement, objectives, strategic goals, and tactical goals with the various types of reengineering projects. Reengineering projects can be defined by their scope, and as illustrated here, by the level of the organization's strategic plan being addressed.

statement have been determined, *strategic goals* are ascertained. Work-flow analysis is the type of reengineering project that would address strategic goals based on objectives for the organization. A strategic goal would provide guidance for satisfying the objectives identified by the organization. Strategic goals are time specific and quantifiable. For example, the previously stated objective might include a strategic goal stated as follows: Increase international market share in Spain by 10 percent for the next three years. This type of quantifiable objective could be accomplished through analyzing specific processes (narrower in scope).

Tactical goals which would further refine strategic goals allow technologies to be applied to specific areas of the organization. Each department would determine tactically, how it could support the strategic goals of the organization. Planning, at all levels of the organization, must directly relate to business reengineering efforts (see Figure 9.6).

CHAPTER HIGHLIGHTS

✎ Continuous improvement is applied to both the outcome or the newly redesigned process as well as to the redesign process itself.

✎ In order to continually improve the outcome or redesigned process, the following must be built into the redesign process itself.

   ◊ Clearly define what the outcome of the redesigned process is.

   ◊ Determine how you will measure whether the redesigned process was successful. Determine the criteria for evaluation.

   ◊ Continuous improvement should be factored into each phase (planning, redesign, transition, and implementation) of the business reengineering project.

✎ Not only does the outcome (redesigned process) need to be assessed and continually improved, the guidelines or methodology for redesigning processes must be continually improved. Once the guidelines are identified and the steps followed, the guidelines themselves must be assessed and fine-tuned in order to provide improved results the next time processes are redesigned.

✎ In order for the outcome to be successful, the methodology used must be customized for the organization, taking into account corporate culture, the history of the organization, and the effect that has on the individuals.

✎ Change management involves many different facets including good leadership. The problem that many organizations have today is the proliferation of managers within the organization at the expense of leaders.

◊ Managers control processes and maintain the status quo. They "manage" the existing environment.

◊ Leaders improve processes, introduce change, in order to move the organization toward a specific goal.

✎ Leaders rather than managers are needed to assist organizations to continually improve and become dynamic, vital organizations within the next century.

✎ In order for change to take effect and be productive, the organizational structure must be positively skewed toward risk-taking and change. Change, for change's sake should be avoided; however, change in order for the organization to survive should become part of the corporate culture.

✎ Change with direction is progress; change without direction is chaos.

✎ Any redesigned processes and changes in general must be linked to the strategic plan of the organization. Change, in this case redesigned processes, must be coordinated and directed toward a common goal.

✎ The vision and direction of the organization should be shared from top management through the ranks to the hourly staff. The objectives of the organization determine which processes should be redesigned. This direction helps provide continuity.

CLOSING THOUGHTS

The following provides a recap of some major thoughts and ideas addressed in this book:

♦ Technology is changing at an ever-increasing rate. Competitive threats exist, not only nationally, but internationally. The playing field has changed and those organizations that are able to adapt quickly will survive and thrive.

♦ The industrial model, with layers of management, is not effective in today's ever-changing world. The role of middle management is changing. Technology has replaced the need for layers of management to filter and summarize information.

♦ In order for businesses to succeed in today's economy, change must be embraced. Doing things the way they have always been done is not effective.

♦ Reengineering means *doing the right things right!*

♦ Technology will play a major role in redesign projects; however, it should not be the driving force. Sound business decisions should drive redesign processes. Technology may enable those changes to take place; however, implementing technology should not be the focal point of any reengineering project

♦ Reengineering projects can be categorized by the scope of the project (technology application, work-flow analysis, business process redesign, and reengineering). All four types of reengineering projects provide improvements to the way things are currently done. However, the broader the scope of the project, the more ability for major changes and therefore major benefits to occur.

♦ It is important to identify the problem or opportunity rather than the symptom. Time should be taken to thoroughly understand the problem and succinctly identify it. Solving symptoms, rather than problems, provides no long-term solution—it is a band aid approach.

♦ Modeling techniques used in information systems development can prove valuable in reengineering projects. If portions of the redesigned process will be automated, models such as data flow diagramming and entity-relationship diagramming can be used by systems analysts as a starting point for developing an automated system. By using the same modeling techniques throughout the reengineering project, communication between team members will be increased, and redundant work will be eliminated.

♦ The guidelines provided in this book constitute a methodology that can be customized by individual organizations to reengineer their processes. A reengineering project consists of four phases—planning, redesign, transition, and implementation.

♦ Team building and staff training are benefits that can be derived from implementing reengineering concepts. As individuals participate in a reengineering project, JIT training can be incorporated into the project.

♦ Reengineering projects should be selected that provide benefit to the organization and support the mission of the institution. The ideal reengineering project will have a low risk of failure and a high payback or return on the time and moneys invested.

♦ Senior management's support and leadership is necessary for the successful completion of business process redesign. Management's acknowledgment that reengineering is a good idea is very different from management's directive that reengineering is the direction the organization should take—critically assessing its internal processes.

Business reengineering done at any level in the organization is not an easy task. Work still needs to be done and current levels of service must be retained during the reengineering project. In some cases, technology can be applied to simple, time-consuming processes in order to free staff time to critically assess their processes. Changing the way things are done is never an easy undertaking. Once the redesigned process is implemented, the change is made, it is not the end. This is a fact that startles many individuals. Any changes to existing processes must be *continually* assessed and modified in order for long-term benefits to be obtained. Organizations that face the challenge and embrace reengineering as a continual process rather than as a static, one-time exercise, will reap the benefits. Once a process is redesigned, it must continually be reassessed, improved, and changed in order to meet changing demands. Those organizations that accept the transition from managing and controlling current processes to changing and adapting to their environment will succeed not only in today's marketplace, but in tomorrow's as well.

PART IV

Techniques and Tools to Help You Redesign Your Processes

What Do You Need to Know to Get Started?

OVERVIEW OF TECHNIQUES USEFUL IN BPR PROJECTS

Within an organization many different techniques can facilitate the process of redesigning projects. The idea of using proven techniques to help with a specific task is not new. Architects use models and builders use blueprints to provide a graphic representation of a completed structure. Information engineers and business process redesigners also use modeling techniques specifically designed for implementing change and modeling information systems such as data flow diagrams, entity-relationship diagrams, flowcharting, and matrices. These techniques originate from various business and computer science disciplines and can be adapted for business process redesign projects.

Modeling Techniques

In many professions modeling has been a proven method for conveying information. Architects model their conceptual ideas of what a building will look like by creating a replica of the building in a miniaturized scale. Engineers use computer models, with the aid of CAD/CAM software, to visualize what an engine or product will look like, how it will relate to other components, and how it will react under certain situations. Models are powerful tools that help you visualize and understand an undeveloped or unconstructed blueprint or plan. Models can also be used to help visualize current and future business processes and information systems. In this sense, the model helps the designer and management alike determine what the scope of the project will be, what departments will be affected, what information will flow within the redesigned process or system, and how all of this will come together in a redesigned business process or system.

Just as no two artists viewing the same landscape draw the same picture, no two business redesigners will model a system or business process in exactly the same way, given the same requirements. Because this is the case, it is imperative that a uniform method of notating one's ideas be determined so that concepts as well as physical details can be communicated between members of a redesign project. A new method of notating ideas could be developed; however, the problem then arises that not everyone understands the notation. If modeling techniques already exist that can be modified and used for business process redesign projects, then why reinvent the wheel? This is the logic behind using existing modeling techniques derived from structured analysis and information engineering techniques. The modeling techniques overviewed in this chapter are data flow diagrams (DFD), entity-relationship diagrams (ERD), flow-charting (or as some methodologies call it "mapping"), and graphics and matrices.

Other modeling techniques used to develop computer information systems include event analysis, decision trees, decomposition diagrams, and structure charts to name a few. These modeling and information-capturing techniques are beyond the scope of this book. They provide detailed specifications for developing a computer information system that is not required during the redesign phase of a BPR project.

BPR projects are divided into four phases: planning, redesign, transition, and implementation. If portions of a BPR project will be implemented using computer information systems, then either internal information systems analysts and programmers or computer programming consultants will provide the necessary design detail to implement those portions. Information systems professionals would use techniques such as event analysis to provide the level of detail required to develop a computer system. High-level DFDs or ERDs provide a starting point for computer systems development. DFDs and ERDs can become quite complicated and detailed; however, they can also be used at a higher level of abstraction. The reason for using DFDs and ERDs to model the processes being redesigned is to allow information systems programmers and analysts the opportunity to use the information gathered in the redesign phase of a BPR project to develop computer information systems if necessary. In this way, redundant work is eliminated. The information captured in the high-level DFD and ERD models created by a BPR team can be used by computer systems professionals as a starting point from which to provide further detailed specification to develop a computer information system.

Data Flow Diagrams (DFD)

Data flow diagramming techniques have been taught in many university computing curriculums. This standard diagramming technique is used in structured systems analysis and design as well as in information engineering techniques. Its widespread popularity is a result of its simplicity. Only four graphical representations are allowed, contrasted to flowcharting which has a myriad of graphical notations. The data flow diagram charts the flow of information within a process or system. These diagrams can model the information flow within a subset of the business (i.e., a specific process or system within the organization as a whole). For example, a DFD can represent the billing process within a company or a DFD of even less detail (higher level of abstraction) can represent the entire organization showing the organization's relationship with areas outside the scope of

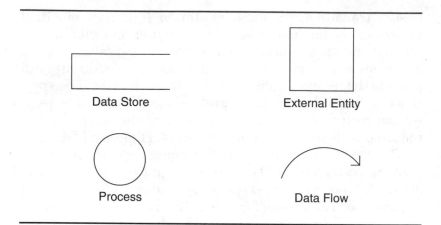

Figure A.1   Data flow diagrams (DFD) consist of four symbols which, when combined according to specific rules, provide a model of an information system or any type of business process. Although DFDs are generally used in structured analysis and information engineering techniques, these models can be useful tools in BPR projects. DFDs used in BPR projects would not contain as much detail, or levels of decomposition, as DFD models used in computer information systems design. However, high-level DFDs can provide an excellent starting point for information systems developers.

the organization such as the government, customers, and banks. Figure A.1 provides an example of each of the graphical notations used in a data flow diagram. Various notation styles have been developed over the years, but two of the most popular are the Yourdon DFD and the Gane-Sarson DFD. Whatever the style used, there are still only four symbols; the difference lies in the notation of the symbols used to represent the four components of a DFD (process, information flow, external entity, and data store).

An in-depth discussion of data flow diagramming uses within computer information systems development, CASE tools, and structure charts and program code preparation is beyond the scope of this book. DFDs are introduced at this time to provide an overview of what a data flow diagram is, its uses in business process redesign projects, and some of the advantages as well as the disadvantages of this type of modeling tool. If you are interested in a detailed explanation of how to model systems using data flow diagrams, a suggested readings list is provided at the end of this appendix. For business redesign projects, the data flow diagram provides a method for modeling what a business process could be. An individual working on a business process redesign project can use this technique at a high level of abstraction (very little detail). A person can use a DFD without knowing the intricacies of decomposing the diagrams to an elementary level of detail. Decomposing the DFD is a process whereby more and more detail is uncovered as each process is investigated further. (An elementary DFD details the point from which actual program logic or procedural manuals could be written.) However, the benefit of using data flow diagrams (DFDs) is that once the essence of what the new system should do is determined, a systems analyst or programmer analyst can use this diagram as a starting point to further decompose it to the level of detail required to generate programming logic. In this way consistency can be maintained between redesigning the process and implementing the changes.

DFDs model a system without regard to time; they do not depict sequential events. In other words, there is no starting point or ending point. Sometimes it is difficult to model a system using data flow diagrams because all functions, regardless of when they occur, must be depicted. A paid bill cannot be sent to a vendor until a bill has been received and the checkbook balance verified. However, the DFD does not show this sequence of events. It depicts the system in a constant state in time when all events could occur. This lack of sequence depiction can be beneficial. If you are trying to determine all of the information required or generated from a specific process or procedure, this is the best modeling technique to capture information. DFDs can be used to model both automated and manual processes.

There are two different types of data flow diagrams. Each contains the same four symbols; however, they represent different aspects of the process or system which they are modeling. The two types of data flow diagrams are the logical or essential model and the physical or transitional model. The essential model shows what the system should do rather than how it will accomplish it. In other words, the essential model lacks any physical details (see Figure A.2). Whether information is stored in a database or in a filing cabinet is not depicted on the essential DFD. What is depicted on the essential DFD is a data store illustrating that certain infor-

Essential versus Transitional DFD	
Essential DFD	*Transitional DFD*
Represents what the system or process does (for example, if the data store contains billing information, the label would indicate this, regardless of whether the store was a database or filing cabinet).	Represents not only what the system will do but also how it will be done (for example, if the data store is a billing database, the label of the data store would indicate this).
Sometimes referred to as the **logical** model of the process or system under consideration.	Sometimes referred to as the **physical** or **implementation** model of the process or system under consideration.
Most used in high-level systems analysis.	Generally used in detailed systems analysis or while designing the new information system.
More likely to be used in a business process redesign project.	Less likely to be used in a business process redesign project.

Figure A.2   There are two different types of DFD (data flow diagrams) that are used during computer systems development. The essential or logical DFD is a useful technique which can be used during business reengineering projects. The transitional or physical model is most useful during the transition or phase of a business reengineering project, since it depicts the physical characteristics of a system or process. Physical characteristics include whether information is stored in an electronic database or in a paper filing cabinet as well as which portions of the process are manual and which are automated.

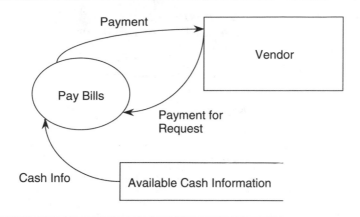

Figure A.3   The essential DFD contains information that logically depicts what the process accomplishes without identifying specific physical character-istics of how it might currently be accomplished. For example, the data store containing available cash information might be labeled as a checkbook in a transitional DFD. The benefit of eliminating what the process does from how it currently does it is a benefit when attempting to rethink business processes.

mation must be stored at a specific point in the system with-out any consideration of the kind of storage—an electronic database or a paper filing cabinet, for example. Figure A.3 provides an example of an essential DFD. Note that the dia-gram lacks any physical characteristics. This is an excep-tionally useful model for business process redesign purposes. It allows a fresh look at what the system should do rather than how it will do it. In many cases, it is difficult to pull the essence of what the system does or should do out of the de-tails of how the system currently works.

Data flow diagrams (DFDs) are also an excellent tech-nique to illustrate a project's scope. The scope of a project affects the type of project it is—work flow, business process redesign, or business reengineering. The data flow diagram, by its very nature, identifies the scope of a project. Whatever is included in the external entities portion of the diagram is beyond the scope of the project. Because of this visual repre-sentation, it is an excellent model to use to determine con-

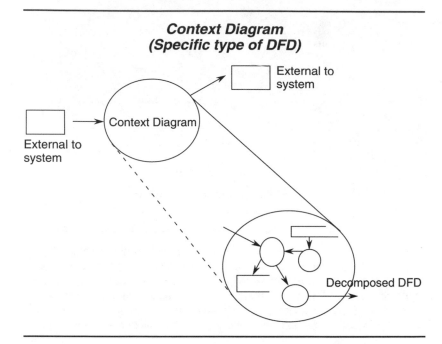

Figure A.4   This specific type of DFD (context diagram) does not show the detail within the system being modeled. The detail would be depicted in a subsequent, more detailed DFD, a decomposed DFD. The context diagram provides a graphical representation of the scope of the project without illustrating all of the detail.

sensus among management and/or participants in the project regarding the scope of a particular project. The context diagram is a specific type of DFD which is used to define the scope of a project. Figure A.4 provides an example of a context diagram.

The physical or transitional DFD, as it is sometimes called, derives from the essential model. This model takes the essence of the system and describes how it will be implemented (see Figure A.5). It differentiates which portion of the system will be automated and which will be manual. It also differentiates which information will be stored and accessible on-line and which will be archived or accessible through batch computing. Automation boundaries, process-

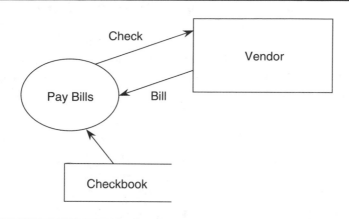

Figure A.5 The physical DFD contains information that depicts not only what the process accomplishes but also how it accomplishes it—specific physical characteristics. Notice the difference between this diagram and Figure A.3. The payment data flow has been renamed to 'check' to illustrate that a physical check is sent. If bills were paid via a computer on-line service then the data flow would indicate a funds transfer. Note what the checkbook and the bill were referred to in the essential DFD model.

ing platforms, and timing considerations (batch versus on-line) are physical characteristics of a system depicted by a transitional DFD. When physical characteristics are being determined, it is necessary for information systems professionals such as internal systems analysts, programmer analysts, or external consultants with a background in systems development to be involved in the process. By using the DFD modeling technique for business process redesign projects, consistency exists between the high-level, essential models used for redesigning business processes and those more detailed and physical models used for implementing systems.

The benefits of using a modeling technique such as data flow diagrams in a BPR project are:

♦ Information shared in a consistent manner with computer systems developers.
♦ Essence of what a newly redesigned business process should accomplish depicted graphically.

♦ A diagram from which consensus among participants can be verified provided.

♦ What the new system should do without knowing up front how it will be accomplished is determined. (Provides an opportunity to view the situation in a new way.)

♦ Model illustrating how various processes interrelate is provided.

Though this modeling technique provides many benefits, it is not a panacea. This diagramming technique does not show timing or sequence of events, as mentioned earlier. It does not provide a complete picture of any process. Even in structured analysis methodologies the data flow diagram does not stand alone. It is coupled with other diagramming tools in order to provide a complete picture of the new system. Entity-relationship diagrams usually go hand-in-hand with data flow diagrams in order to provide a more robust model of the new system.

Entity-relationship Diagrams (ERD)

Entity-relationship diagrams are another technique used extensively in information systems development. Structured analysis, as well as information engineering techniques, use this type of model to graphically represent a system. (Object-oriented methodologies also use a variation of this type of diagramming technique.) The entity-relationship diagram visually depicts the relationship between various "things" within a system. The things or entities which are being modeled can be anything about which information needs to be captured. In other words, an entity can be a person, place, thing, or event. Examples of entities include CUSTOMER, INVOICE, PRODUCT. Figure A.6 illustrates how entities relate to one another.

Entity-relationship diagrams contain even fewer symbols than data flow diagrams. Again, there are various styles of notation such as Chen, Bachman, and Martin style entity-relationship diagrams. The examples used in this book follow the Martin style of entity-relationship diagramming.

Concept of Entity-relationship Diagram

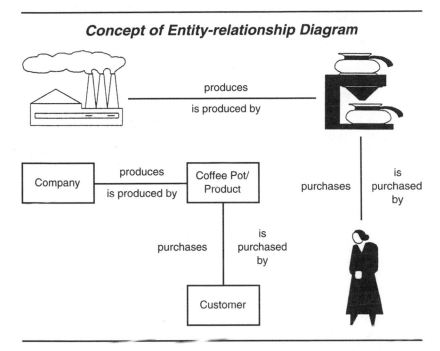

Figure A.6 These diagrams represent the relationship between a company, product, and customer. Entity-relationship diagrams (data models) do not usually contain pictures such as those shown here because of the difficulty in drawing. However, the same information is conveyed whether you use a picture to represent a customer or a rectangle labeled with the word customer. An entity-relationship diagram is a model used to depict the data being captured and stored by an organization. The same information is conveyed in both diagrams.

The differences between these various diagramming styles is not in what they depict, but in the specific notation used to convey the information. For example, the relationship between two entities may be depicted by a straight line or it may be shown with a triangle separating the entities. In either case, the meaning of the model is the same; the only difference is in the type of symbol or notation used. Figure A.7 contains ERD notation used in the Martin style. Entity-relationship modeling is used to illustrate the entities, or what information needs to be captured about them, and their relationships with each other. For instance, an entity-rela-

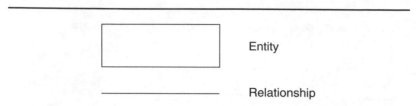

Entity

Relationship

There are only two symbols used in the Martin style ERD. There is additional notation which is used to depict cardinality and optionality, discussed with the next diagram.

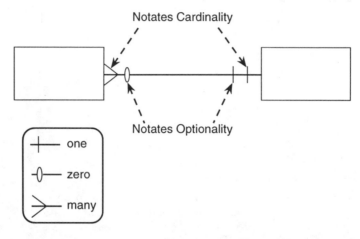

Optionality notes whether the relationship is optional. The choices for noting optionality are **one** or **zero**. One indicates that it is not optional and zero indicates that it is optional. Cardinality notes whether the relationship can contain only **one** or **many**. For example, the diagram in Figure A.6 contains a relationship between Product and Customer which could be depicted as follows:

The product can be purchased by zero (optionality) or many (cardinality) customers. The customer can purchase one (optionality) or many (cardinality) products. Both optionality and cardinality determine the type of relationship between two entities.

Figure A.7   ERD notation used in the Martin style.

tionship diagram would illustrate the relationship between a customer and an invoice. This technique is used extensively in information engineering projects. It can also be used at a higher level of abstraction within business process redesign projects. Entity-relationship diagrams, like DFDs, can provide broad, high-level information or very specific, detailed information. Like data flow diagrams, entity-relationship diagrams can capture general information in the redesign phase of a project and pass that information on to programmers or systems analysts as a starting point for gathering more detailed information.

Entity-relationship modeling is a useful technique in business process redesign because it focuses on the information required by a specific process or set of processes and does not concentrate on how things are currently being done. Because of the emphasis on data rather than process, ERDs can help redesigners break out of the current "it's always been done this way" mold and look at the process in a new light. Entity-relationship diagrams can be used to depict the logical representation between entities within a specific system or they can be used to help develop a database schema. (A database schema is a detailed model of how the database will be structured and is the type of information a computer systems analyst would provide.) For purposes of BPR projects, the entity-relationship diagrams would be used to show the relationship between entities rather than the detailed ERDs necessary to produce a database schema. Before a schema for a database could be produced, the data represented by the entities would need to be normalized. Normalizing data and developing a database schema should be done by internal IS professionals or external consultants experienced with this type of automated systems development. The benefit of using ERDs to describe relationships between entities in a system or process is similar to the benefit of using DFD models. The information captured and notated in the ERD models can be given to systems designers and programmers to detail further and create a database schema to implement the automated portions of the redesigned business process. Information will not be lost in the translation from one model or set of notations to another.

Flowcharting (Mapping)

Flowcharting is a technique with which every programmer or analyst is familiar. It is also the technique most non-IS professionals relate to information system development and programming. However, it is not used in modern structured analysis because other tools have replaced it to depict program logic. Decision tables, decision trees, pseudo code, N-S diagrams, and action diagrams have replaced the flow chart in information systems development. However, many other disciplines have picked up this technique—it is sometimes referred to as "mapping." Additional symbols may be added; however, the concept remains the same. The idea of calling this technique mapping derives from translating functions and steps within a business process and relating them graphically, or mapping them. Some total quality management programs use this technique to determine value-added and nonvalue-added steps within a process (see Figure A.8). A value-added step in a process is one that directly provides a benefit to the ultimate customer of the process. For example, in a retail store operation a procedure requiring that a customer fill out a form before talking with a customer service clerk would be a nonvalue-added step. The procedure may have been instituted because it alleviated some of the paperwork necessary by the back office employees. However, it is necessary to focus on what steps or procedures in a business process directly correlate to a benefit to the customer.

Mapping is a useful technique for projects which have a limited scope—by definition, work-flow projects. It can be used by specific departments in an organization to help them reduce unnecessary steps in a given limited-scope project without redesigning the entire process. This technique is not useful for modeling a system where business reengineering or business redesign is involved because it maps or

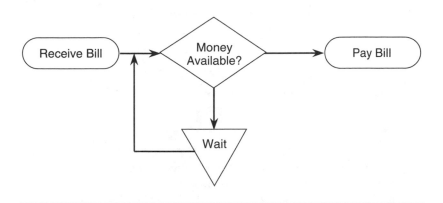

Figure A.8 This diagram is a simplified example of a map. Mapping techniques vary; however, they use many of the symbols formerly used to develop flow charts. One noted difference is the addition of a wait state added to the map. The map is used to show, from a customer's perspective, the steps necessary to complete a process, including any waiting periods. The map or flow chart illustrates the sequence of events (remember data flow diagrams did not show sequence). This is a very useful technique for eliminating nonvalue added steps when the scope of a project is small enough. Mapping should be done for technology application and work-flow projects.

depicts the current situation, not what *should be done*. However, it can be a useful technique to assist in understanding specific nuances of a process or system. Don't try to use it to model an entire system that is being redesigned. The map will be too long and will not serve any useful purpose.

Graphics and Matrices

A picture is worth a thousand words. DFDs and ERDs model processes and systems. Matrices provide tabular information while graphs, such as pie charts, bar charts, and trend charts depict tabular information in graphical format. Anytime a matrix or graph can be used to illustrate existing relationships or trends, it should be. Information engineering techniques use matrices extensively. This technique

Matrix Example

	Personnel	Payroll	Benefits
Hire Personnel	X	X	X
Reclassify Job Positions	X		
Reassign Personnel	X	X	

Figure A.9 Matrices can be used to show the relationship between any two items. This example shows the relationship between functions and departments. This technique provides a clearer understanding of the relationship between any two items.

lends itself particularly well to business process redesign projects. Matrices can be used to illustrate the relationship between departments in an organization and functions performed, or between functions performed and corporate goals. Matrices can depict the relationship between any two things or entities in an organization (see Figure A.9). The most difficult part of using this technique is determining what two things should be related in order to provide useful information for the business process redesign project.

MODELING VERIFICATION TECHNIQUES

After models have been developed, whether they are a DFD, ERD, map, or matrix, they need to be verified for accuracy. Inspecting or auditing your work for accuracy has always been a viable validation technique. However, even after models have been inspected or audited, information may still be missing or notation problems may exist. Two very useful validation techniques are used in structured analysis and information engineering for ensuring validation of these models. They are the walkthrough and the joint requirements planning (JRP) session. These validation techniques can be used in BPR projects quite effectively.

Walkthrough

The walkthrough is a structured analysis technique that is used to validate DFD and ERD models. However, the concept of a walkthrough can be used to validate any type of information. It is a technique that facilitates understanding between the participants of the walkthrough. There are two types or variations of this technique—peer or technical walkthrough, and a general or requirements validation walkthrough. A technical walkthrough is a structured meeting composed of individuals who developed the model and their peers. In this context, peers are any individuals who understand the modeling techniques and associated notations, but they do not have to understand the system or process being modeled. In fact, it is preferred that they are unfamiliar with the system being modeled since they may raise questions or issues not previously uncovered because of the designer's familiarity with the system. The focus will then be on the model itself.

The purpose of the walkthrough, even after individuals believe their models to be complete, is to find ways to enhance the model or correct omissions and problems the developer or designer did not see. People feel uncomfortable with this concept. It is human nature to want to present work you have done and have your peers congratulate you. It takes a different mind set to create a successful walkthrough. Everyone must be comfortable with openly and constructively criticizing the model. Remember, the purpose of a walkthrough is to improve the model at a point in the redesign process when changes can easily be made. It is a lot easier to change the location of a door to a house on the blueprint then it is to change the location of the door after the house has been built.

In addition to technical walkthroughs, there are general walkthroughs which attempt to ascertain the validity of the model's ability to represent the process being modeled. In a general walkthrough the developer of the model, and the management and staff working in the functional areas of the business meet. The purpose of this type of walkthrough is to determine the representational validity of the model. In other words, does it represent *what* the system or process either does or should do? Essential DFD and ERD models, validated in this way, determine if all the requirements of the process have been captured. In the building trades, a contractor will have several walkthroughs with his client while the house is being built. You may walk through the house when only the floor or foundation is laid, prior to any walls being built, in order to verify or validate the location of the interior walls. After the walls are up, you may walk through your new home so the builder can verify the location of the doors, closets, and windows. Then a final walkthrough precedes your final payment for the house.

This same walkthrough scenario should be followed when redesigning business processes. Though no physical building or structure exists to walk through, the concept is the same. The business process redesigner would sit down with the management and staff of the areas affected by the redesign and explain the model to them—walk them through the model. Just as the builder is looking for feedback from his client before the entire house is built—when it is easy to make the changes—the business process redesigner is looking for changes or new requirements not previously revealed. The walkthrough process also serves to validate that the model represents what the process should accomplish.

Walkthroughs assume that the model has been drawn by someone other than the people working in the functional areas, that is the departments affected by the change or redesign. Information systems have typically been developed in the past by programmers or analysts without full involvement from the users. Users were necessary to determine what the system being developed should do; however, this was generally accomplished through interviews, questionnaires, observations, and walkthroughs. New emphasis is being placed on end-user involvement in the information system development process. For business process redesign projects, people affected by the change must play an active role in making the change. JRP sessions have become more prevalent in information systems development because of the degree of end-user involvement. Joint requirements planning is a core technique necessary in successful business process redesign projects.

Joint Requirements Planning (JRP) Session

Joint requirements planning (JRP) sessions derive from JAD (joint applications development) sessions. JAD sessions have become prevalent in the development of modern information systems. JRP (joint requirements planning) sessions can be used to validate models previously prepared by the business process redesigner, or they can be used to develop the models themselves in a team environment. If a model is developed in a JRP session, validation is still required following the JRP session. If JRP sessions are not used to develop the models, then interviews, questionnaires, or audits and observations are techniques the business process redesigner must use to determine the scope of the project and how the process currently works as well as what is required to be done. The emphasis should not be placed on *how* things are currently done; however, the current system must be understood at a higher conceptual level in order to discuss *what* the system or process should do. There may be certain procedures which must be retained, even if major changes are desired. The benefits of using a JRP session to develop a model rather than the business process redesigner's personally developed model are as follows:

♦ Less overall time spent.
♦ More involvement of functional business area staff in redesign process.
♦ Information will be shared. Staff may discover information from other staff members they were unaware of that may not be disclosed through the business process redesigner's modeling of the system.
♦ Facilitates breakthrough thinking.

Joint requirements planning (JRP) or joint application development (JAD) techniques are useful tools in a business process redesign project. In a meeting or series of meetings, everyone is involved in redesigning the processes and in determining requirements or the design of the new system. Business area managers and staff need to dedicate a substantial portion of their time during this process. Therefore, senior management commitment must be obtained at the beginning of the project. The benefits of this technique far outweigh the additional time constraints on the business area's management and staff. The overall elapsed time of the project is condensed by this approach even though more meetings and more people attending each meeting are required. Less time means less resources spent on the project and ultimately less cost. It also means the changes are implemented sooner, allowing the company to take advantage of the redesigned systems before their competition.

REDESIGN TECHNIQUES

Techniques for modeling have been discussed as well as various methods for validating the models. But, how does the development of valid models help redesign a business process? The answer is that the techniques, on their own, will not provide any breakthrough thinking or major redesign alternatives. However, using these techniques in conjunction with various management techniques will assist individuals to break out of their paradigms and become most effective.

Breakthrough Thinking

Breakthrough thinking is simply a way to think about a problem or process that has not been done before, such as looking at a situation or an issue from a different perspective. This is difficult to do, and is rarely accomplished by a single person sitting alone thinking about a problem. Breakthrough thinking usually occurs when a group of individuals, all with different perspectives of a problem, come together to discuss options. Diversity of the members involved in a breakthrough thinking session is a real asset. If everyone has an open mind and really listens to the views and ideas of others, extraordinary results can be accomplished. The key point is if everyone has an open mind. Prior to the beginning of the session it is imperative that the tone be set. In order for any new ideas to occur the environment must be conducive to risk-taking. People must feel comfortable making suggestions without fear of repercussion or humiliation. There are various techniques which can be used to facilitate breakthrough thinking, a few of which follow.

Brainstorming

Brainstorming has been defined in many different ways; however, for our purposes it is a technique which allows new solutions and ideas to be identified and defined in the context of a meeting. The strength of brainstorming lies in its ability to consolidate and build upon the ideas of several individuals. In order for a brainstorming session to be productive the participants must be able to view the existing process in different ways. *Use of brainstorming and other breakthrough thinking techniques discussed here is the core of business process redesign.* If new ways to do business are not incorporated into the newly designed systems, major benefits will not be achieved. It will not matter how well modeling techniques were used.

You want to be sure not to automate existing processes which no longer effectively serve the organization. Business process redesign can use the techniques used by structured analysis and information engineering techniques; however, the element of changing the way business is done must be present. Otherwise, the same type of systems development will continue under a new name. The process of developing new systems, whether automated or manual, must consolidate the strengths of structured analysis, information engineering, and management concepts such as total quality management and continuous improvement in order for significant changes to take place. Brainstorming and other breakthrough thinking techniques allow significant changes in the way business is conducted to occur.

Brainstorming has certain rules which need to be adhered to in order to produce successful results. Personal attacks or attacking someone's idea is prohibited. Comments such as "that's a stupid idea" are not tolerated in a brainstorming session. The purpose is to generate as many ideas and the wildest ideas in order to provide individuals with the opportunity to build upon those ideas or any part of them. Another rule or guideline for brainstorming sessions is that they should be facilitated by an objective individual, not one involved in the outcome of the session. This allows for objectivity and the necessity of keeping the session on track. Usually a time limit is determined prior to the brainstorming session. An organization can fine-tune this technique to meet its needs. Established guidelines for a brainstorming session should be communicated to participants prior to the session. The participants should feel comfortable enough with the rules, colleagues in the session, and the topic, to freely express ideas and thoughts, even though they may think their initial ideas are unusual. The unusual, wild, or crazy ideas are usually the ones that spark creativity within the participants of the brainstorming session and ultimately result in a solution or redesigned system that would not have been discovered otherwise.

Double Reversal

Double reversal is a type of brainstorming technique. Sometimes asking individuals to provide solutions or ideas for a new process does not generate any new ideas. Double reversal asks the question, "How could you redesign this process to be the most cumbersome for customers, time-consuming for employees, or cost the greatest amount of money?" After several ideas on how to redesign the process with the worst possible solution, the emphasis of the session shifts. The session starts with the reverse goal of making the system the worst possible system, but the session ends by reversing the goal again—the best possible system. By taking the ideas generated on how to make the system the worst, the participants sort through the ideas to determine if there are any ideas that were generated which, if reversed, could improve the system or totally redesign it to increase customer satisfaction, save time for employees, or save money.

Probing

Sometimes it is difficult for individuals to break out of their paradigms. The outcome of brainstorming sessions may be the inability to see other ways to accomplish a specific function or process within the organization. At these times it is useful to probe further to determine why no alternatives are readily thought of. Asking a series of "whys"—why is something done a certain way or why can't it be done differently—is a useful technique to uncover the underlying rationale for an existing process or function. Consequently, this technique uncovers personal concerns, political realities, and cultural issues within the organization, that are prohibitive to change. Begin questioning or probing by asking why the process or function should exist at all. After a reason is given, ask if the reason is valid. Usually five to six levels of "why" questioning will uncover the underlying *reason* why individuals feel there are no ways to radically change what is being done. Sometimes political reasons are the underlying cause why resistance to change exists. Sometimes it is just difficult for people to get past the boundaries that are currently set by the existing process. But it is wise to announce this technique to the group prior to questioning their responses. People can feel threatened if they think you are questioning why they have responded to you in a certain manner and you have not accepted their answer; but continue to question them. This is also a useful technique to uncover possible reasons why individuals may be resistant to a proposed change.

JIT Training

Modeling techniques, validation issues, and breakthrough thinking concepts have been discussed. How are individuals going to participate in a business process redesign project when they need all of this knowledge? You could set up training classes and have the participants work on case studies and use the modeling techniques as they study the various concepts. However, this is time-consuming and, after all of the training classes are completed, you are still not guaranteed that the trained individuals will be able to apply the concepts they learned to a redesign project. A more suitable approach is to provide them with just-in-time (JIT) training. This approach builds the training into the actual project.

For example, rather than having a training session teaching individuals how to model using DFDs and ERDs and then, maybe months later asking them to work on a redesign project to model proposed changes, why not teach them the modeling techniques they need to know while they are modeling the process under consideration? The concept of JIT training is similar to apprenticeships. People would be taught what they need to know while they are actually performing the task. Many companies are looking at the concept of JIT training for various needs. Building the training into the project will extend each phase of the project slightly; however, participants' retention of the material learned will increase. Most of what is learned in a classroom setting is lost before it can be applied. With JIT training both learning and application of the learned skill are almost instantaneous.

JIT training could be built into a business process redesign (BPR) project at various phases. Training could be done at the beginning of the project to cover concepts and introduce the project as an overview. It is important to place the right person in the role of team leader if JIT training techniques will be used. The trainer does not need to be the team leader; in fact, it is preferred if the trainer isn't. However, the team leader needs to support the learning process and keep the project on schedule. A balance between learning and applying the learned skill must be successfully accomplished. DFD and ERD or other modeling techniques should not be introduced until participants are ready to model the redesigned system. Team building is another skill that could be introduced as JIT training during the BPR project, since the participants will be working as a team to redesign a specific business process. The use of JIT training in the organization is limited only by your imagination!

APPENDIX A HIGHLIGHTS

✎ Using techniques and models in redesigning business processes is a procedure that has been used in many disciplines. Architects have always modeled proposed buildings and builders have used blueprints (graphical representations of the model) to build them. Business process redesigners can use DFDs and ERDs, as well as other modeling techniques, and systems integrators or developers can build an automated system from those models. Work completed by the BPR team can be easily transferred to the programmers and systems analysts to develop computer information systems or apply technologies to the redesigned processes. The essential question arises—Is this process necessary? Does the technology enable change or is the manual process being mimicked by the technology? An example of mimicking manual processes without making radical changes to the underlying business functions can be illustrated by certain applications of imaging technology used to route forms through the organization. If the actual form is electronically routed from workstation to workstation, has anything really changed? The medium has changed—digitized information rather than paper is being routed. But have any major breakthroughs occurred? Has the process been redesigned or simply automated?

✎ If you are interested in further information regarding the techniques discussed in this appendix, particularly the DFD and ERD modeling techniques, the following list of books will prove useful (full bibliographic information is given in the References at the end of the book):

James Martin, *Information Engineering*, Book I.

James Martin, *Information Engineering*, Book II.

James Martin, *Information Engineering*, Book III.

Whitten, Bentley, & Barlow, *Systems Analysis and Design*, 3rd ed.

What Types of Technologies Are Available to Help Redesign Processes?

OVERVIEW OF ENABLING TECHNOLOGIES

Just as there are many techniques that can facilitate BPR projects, there are many tools which can enable the redesigned systems to be implemented. Technologies have allowed us to implement the impossible. For instance, 50 years ago, before the advent of wireless communications and the information superhighway concept, a mobile work force was unheard of. People had to live within commuting distance of their jobs. However, with today's technologies the virtual office is a reality. Sales representatives or executives can work from virtually anywhere in the world. Technology is changing the definition of work and forcing us to rethink the office concept. The fact remains that technology can enable us to implement new ideas.

The danger of these advances lies in automating or applying technology to inefficient or unnecessary processes. Technology applied to a business process is only as beneficial as the logic behind the process itself. If you apply current technology to ineffective processes, you have not achieved any substantial benefits. The individuals who spent all of their time and effort producing buggy whips more efficiently missed the underlying changes that were occurring at the time the automobile was introduced and gaining popularity. Rather than analyzing whether they should even be making buggy whips, all of their effort went into efficiently producing the buggy whip. You can apply technology to efficiently produce the buggy whip; however, if the horse-drawn carriage becomes obsolete, what benefit is derived from fine-tuning the process of making buggy whips? The same analogy holds true for business processes. You must first rethink the business process and then determine if there is a technology that will enable you to implement your redesigned process.

The educational sector has been going through major changes just as business has. With funding being reduced by the states, public education has been forced to cut back. Up to this point, most of the cutbacks have been made in the traditional sense: reduced spending on new equipment, reduced raises for faculty and staff and, in some cases, reduction of programs. However, if substantial savings and changes are to be made, the underlying concept and associated processes must redefine education and learning. Technology can be applied to learning; however, should it augment or replace the classroom as it is defined today? Understanding *what* needs to be accomplished is imperative before applying any technologies to the situation.

TYPES OF ENABLING TECHNOLOGIES

The list of the types of enabling technologies discussed in this section is not an exhaustive one, but it provides a broad overview of current technologies being used to implement business process redesign changes (see Figure B.1). Without many of these technologies, the changes taking place in businesses all over America and the world, for that matter, would not be possible. Currently, available technology allows the redesign of business functions and reorganization of departmental structures. The emphasis, however, must remain on the business processes. *Technology should not drive change; it should enable it.* It is tempting to simply apply the latest

Technology	What is it?
Imaging	Imaging consists of scanning graphics and photographs into digitized format for display on a computer or recognizing typed text and converting it to a word processing format (OCR).
Multimedia	Multimedia combines audio, visual, and textual information to present information or ideas. It is currently being applied as a learning tool for educational institutions as well as corporate training programs.
Work-flow, Groupware	Work-flow software allows documents or information to be routed within an organization. Groupware software allows people to work simultaneously on projects regardless of their physical location.
Client/Server	In a client/server environment the data generallly resides on a database server and various personal computers (clients) access the data in different ways. This allows redesigned processes to be implemented using different program interfaces for different users.
GUI	The graphical user interface (GUI) environment provides a more powerful interface for computer users allowing individuals who may not have used a computer before to be productive sooner.
End-user Computing Trend	Computer users are becoming more empowered—more in control of their own information in order to keep pace with ever-changing business needs. Powerful end-user query tools (programs) reduce the need for traditional computer programming support.

(continued on next page)

Technology	What is it?
Object-oriented Development	Object-oriented development includes not only object-oriented programming languages, but also new ways and methodologies to assist in analyzing and designing computer information systems.
Wireless and Mobile Computing	Wireless and mobile computing allow information to be accessible from anywhere. The constraints of an office do not have to be taken into account when redesigning business processes.
Information Highway	The Internet is the main lane of the information highway. Through the Internet files can be transferred, remote computers can be logged onto, and electronic mail can be sent and received.
Converging Technologies	Voice, data, and graphical imaging are converging. Telephone, electronic mail, and pager systems can be combined into an integrated solution to a redesign process.

Figure B.1   Types of enabling technologies.

technology to current business problems, hoping to correct them. However, it has been proven that applying technology to ineffective processes will only speed up or multiply the ineffectiveness. You will have efficient ineffective processes which is an oxymoron. Efficiency relates to correctly completing a process or task using the least amount of time, the least amount of effort, and the least amount of cost. Effectiveness, on the other hand, addresses the issue of focusing on the correct processes or tasks, those that relate directly to the business of the organization. Efficiency and effectiveness seem to go hand-in-hand. However, you can definitely automate a process and make it as efficient as possible without making it effective. Efficiency does not guarantee effectiveness. Business process redesign can be stated simply as: *Doing the right things right.*

Both efficiency and effectiveness must be addressed simultaneously. An efficient process may have been in place to produce the best buggy whip, but if people are using automobiles instead of horse-drawn carriages, it isn't very effective. Automobiles did not require buggy whips, no matter how efficiently they were produced, and how high the quality or low the cost. Questions must be asked before applying technologies to a problem. If mass production technologies were applied to the production of the buggy whip, more would have been produced in less time. The consequences for the owners would have been even more devastating. They would have had a larger inventory of a useless product.

Before determining if bar coding or mobile computing would provide the most efficient form of inventory tracking, you must determine if you even need to keep an inventory. Maybe outsourcing would be a viable solution, or maybe a new form of inventory management such as JIT inventory control or kanban would be an effective alternative. (*Kanban* is a paperless system, using dedicated containers and mobile requisition cards to keep track of inventory.) The point is that you need to explore all options and define exactly *what* you want to do before you evaluate technologies. After you have determined *what* you want your redesigned process to accomplish you can then ascertain *how* best to implement those changes. When determining which technology would be of the most benefit to a particular redesigned process, seek assistance from either your internal IS staff or outside consultants. You want someone familiar with the various technologies and an understanding of how those technologies could enable your redesigned process to be implemented. Following are some of the current technologies which could enable major changes in business processes if applied correctly.

Imaging

Imaging technology has been around for awhile. Applications were designed to mimic the manual flow of paper in an organization when it was first introduced. A paper form would be scanned into a computer system and routed to various members of the organization to sequentially work on the document. The medium changed from paper to electronic format, but the underlying business process remained the same. Some benefits did arise from this type of application, such as the reduction in lost forms, the reduction of elapsed time between individuals working on the form, and the increased ability to locate the form. However, major changes and major benefits did not occur. Once the document was in electronic form, it could be worked on simultaneously; the document could be cataloged in a database and portions of the manual tasks performed on the document automated. However, many of the earlier imaging applications mimicked the manual processes and routed the document through the organization sequentially—not taking full advantage of the technology. In order to redesign processes to take advantage of any technology, in this case imaging technology, changes in underlying business processes must occur first.

Imaging systems and their associated applications have expanded considerably since their inception. Today imaging systems consist of various types of peripheral devices and applications software. Bar coding as well as desktop publishing and graphics retouching are forms of imaging technology. Scanning and optical character recognition (OCR) have improved tremendously over the past years. Many OCR applications now boast accuracy rates of 95 percent to 97 percent character recognition. Imaging systems can now capture information and place it in a central database repository for use with various application programs and end-user query tools. Graphic images, both still and motion, have begun populating corporate databases. Human resources applications have been developed which provide an image of applicants and employees along with pertinent information. Imaging technology has begun to merge with audio and multimedia is becoming a viable technology for industry and education alike. Imaging technology can enable manual document processing tasks to be radically changed. It can also be used to automate existing processes. Before applying this or any technology to a business problem or opportunity, carefully ascertain the effectiveness of the underlying business process.

Multimedia

Multimedia merges audio, video, graphics, and text within a computer application. Stated in simple terms, multimedia is a method of conveying information in multiple media formats. In order to take advantage of this technology, certain hardware and software are necessary. Computers must be equipped with additional hardware, such as sound boards, in order to take advantage of sound within a multimedia application. Most multimedia applications are distributed on CD-ROMs making a CD-ROM drive another hardware requirement. Multimedia applications have begun to appear in educational settings, such as schools and corporate training programs. Many applications, including Microsoft's Excel and Word have multimedia extensions built-in to them, allowing the attachment of voice messages or recordings to a spreadsheet or word processing document transmitted across the network or diskette. Another technology which uses multimedia to its fullest extent is virtual reality.

Virtual reality seeks to create an environment that does not exist outside of the computer. It is a form of multimedia in which an individual is encompassed by sight, sound, and touch. Flight simulators used by the major airlines provide pilot training through the use of multimedia and virtual reality applications. Corporations which provide training to staff geographically dispersed around the globe can distribute custom training programs based on multimedia. This technology allows distributed training to provide not only instruction, but also verbal and visual feedback, and encouragement. Computer-based training (CBT) programs have been available for some time; however, the current trend of incorporating multimedia capability into these applications is increasing learning retention. It has been known for some time that people learn in different ways. Multimedia technology used in training allows the learner to choose the most comfortable method of learning—audio, visual, or textual.

Virtual reality is a new technology which is currently being applied to education and entertainment. However, there are other applications for this technology, such as providing a means for physically impaired individuals to interact more easily with a computer environment in order to convey their ideas, as well as to provide a productive work environment. Though multimedia and virtual reality are generally applied to individual use; they can be incorporated into a system in which individuals can interact with one another. Groupware computing provides the technical means for individuals to work together, whether multimedia capabilities are available.

Work-flow, Groupware

Work-flow and groupware are technologies which allow people to work in teams and share information. Lotus Notes is an example of groupware software. Specific applications can be built using Lotus Notes which provide custom solutions to business problems. Microsoft also has a work group version of its windows software. Work-group computing allows teams to share information and distribute tasks, whether they are sitting next to each other or across the country. This technology allows people to work as a true team, eliminating duplication of effort and work. Again, the technology is only as viable as the business processes to which it is applied.

Work-flow software provides automation of basic tasks within a business process. Business processes, once redesigned, consist of many work flows. This type of technology can implement redesigned tasks performed at a clerical or knowledge worker level. Work-flow software allows routine forms routing to be automated, capturing valuable information which can be compiled into reports for analysis. Some products that use the work-flow concept include JetForm and PerForm which capture information from a computer screen, store it centrally and, according to specific rules, distribute the information throughout the organization. This technology is useful in automating forms completion and routing within an organization. However, before this type of technology is applied to an organization, the underlying processes determining why certain forms are completed and routed to specific areas should be analyzed. It is possible, and most likely probable, that some forms may be eliminated or redesigned before automation. Work-flow systems generally allow information to be electronically distributed either within or between organizations. Some work-flow software applications incorporate imaging technologies. Many of the technologies discussed here can be implemented concurrently and may depend on each other to efficiently and effectively implement redesigned business processes.

Client/Server

Client/server technology is one of the latest panaceas in the computer industry. Client/server technology usually replaces legacy systems which have been developed on mainframe systems. There are many types of client/server configurations and many definitions of what client/server computing actually is. Client/server technology, no matter how defined, always has two components—a client application and a server application.

The most accepted definition and example of client/server technology is a database server with various client applications accessing the data. For example, a local network could have a database server running a database engine such as Oracle or Sybase. On the client side, the personal computers attached to the network enable workers at their desktops to access that database through custom-developed programs or through products such as Excel (see Figure B.2).

The difference between client/server technology and mainframe technology is that the client, or personal com-

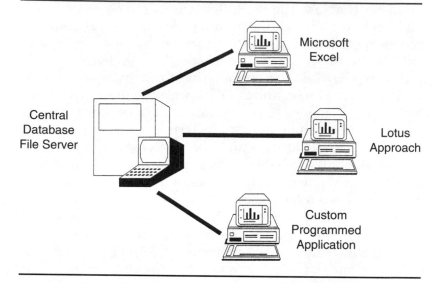

Figure B.2 In a client/server environment a database server can service multiple clients running different software. In this example, one end user could access the database using a Microsoft Excel spreadsheet, while another could use a Lotus Approach database query applicaiton. The client portion of this technology usually consists of software on a personal computer. The server portion can be a high-end personal computer, a minicomputer, or mainframe running the appropriate server software.

puter at the desktop, contains intelligence and requests information or services from the server. In the mainframe environment dumb terminals, which have none or limited intelligence, are attached to a central computer which houses not only the database but appropriate applications as well. In this type of environment, anyone accessing the mainframe data would do so with the same type of interface. The flexibility of allowing computer users to view the data in the manner they are most comfortable with is not available. Various types of servers can be attached to a network, such as database servers, file servers, fax servers, or mail servers, to name a few (see Figure B.3).

If redesigned processes are implemented using client/ server technology, internal programming staff will need to

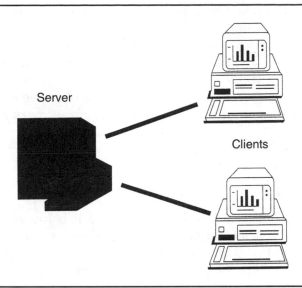

Figure B.3 In a client/server environment a server can service multiple clients. The client portion of this technology is usually a personal computer. The server portion can be a high-end personal computer, a minicomputer, or mainframe. It is depicted here as a generic black box to illustrate that any powerful machine can be used in this capacity. The server may be a database server; however, it may be serving files, mail, faxes, etc. to clients on the network.

be retrained. Developing applications in a client/server environment is very different from developing mainframe COBOL programs accessed by dumb terminals. Portions of the application reside on the server and portions reside on the client, or the desktop personal computer. This technology allows different individuals or departments in an organization to access the same data with different interfaces. The accounting department may want to view and update information in the central database using a spreadsheet program. If they are familiar with spreadsheet applications, little or no training will be required. Executives may want to view information in a graphical format, updated automatically when changes are made. The human resources department may want an application which allows them to fill in a representation of a form on the screen or scan in an application and automatically load it into the database. Client/server technology allows various interfaces to be developed around a central database repository. This provides more flexibility in the way a computer user can view company data. It also provides more technical challenges for the IS staff and may require retraining of programmers and systems analysts. This is a powerful technology that can allow changes in underlying business processes to occur.

Graphical User Interface (GUI)

The graphical user interface or GUI as it is known in computer jargon, is a windows type of interface such as Microsoft Windows, Macintosh, and Motif, as well as others. Many people associate GUI with client/server technology. Although most client/server implementations take advantage of a graphical user interface, it is not a requirement of client/server technology. Graphical user interfaces are frequently provided without client/server technology. GUI environments depict icons or pictures on the computer screen. These represent some function of the programs. For example, an icon containing the picture of a printer when clicked will print the appropriate information. The use of a mouse is assumed when using a GUI. The graphical nature of the interface allows users to manipulate and customize their own environments. This type of interface is more intuitive in nature than traditional character-based environments.

The main advantage of a graphical environment or user interface is its ability to empower the user. Once an individual learns a windows-based application, the functionality of other windows programs is more readily learned. Software developers are focusing more attention on providing a consistent user interface design. The consistency allows an individual's learning curve to be reduced. Exploration is also encouraged in this type of environment, allowing individuals to begin using the basics of an application almost immediately and adding functionality as the user feels more comfortable with the application. For instance, you can start using a GUI word processor almost immediately to type a simple letter and print it. You do not need to understand how to create a table, merge database files into a form letter, or develop a two-column newsletter with graphics to use the application for simple tasks. However, the functionality is built into the application and ready for use when the individual feels comfortable. Most GUIs are customizable which means that individuals can customize their own interface in order to feel more comfortable with a specific application, and ultimately to be more productive. For example, you can create special templates for form letters or change icons which appear on toolbars within programs.

End-user Computing Trend

A major trend in information systems development is the shift from *centrally* controlled and developed systems to *end-user* controlled and developed systems. Using centrally developed systems, programming requests were given to the information systems department or outsourced, and programs were written. When business needs changed, a change request or new program was requested. The problem with this scenario is that factors affecting business are changing more rapidly than traditionally programmed information systems can be revised. The trend is moving away from these centrally developed systems to a centrally maintained database, or data warehouse concept, accessible by various departments and individuals within the organization. Disk operating system DOS-based applications, Windows, and Macintosh may all exist on a common network. Users should be able to access corporate data from any desktop platform, using whatever type of interface with which they are comfortable.

Technology trends such as GUI and client/server are used extensively when developing systems that provide more control of how the data is accessed for the computer user rather than the central IS staff. Software standards and support issues such as training and trouble-shooting are of concern.

However, computer users are becoming more sophisticated and demanding more services and access to more information. Security and data integrity issues are of great priority and need to be maintained centrally; however, departments are empowered to control their own portions of the database and are able to create their own views of the information with assistance from internal IS staff or outside consultants.

This IS trend synchronizes with the management trend of business process redesign. As business processes are re-evaluated and redesigned, the information systems supporting those processes are revamped in order to provide the departments and ultimate users of data more control over their information systems. Coordination of effort must exist in order to ensure that all facets of the organization are pulling in the same direction. The convergence of these two trends provides a great deal of opportunity to redesign processes, and effectively and efficiently implement those changes, both manual and automated, within an organization.

Object-oriented Development

Objected-oriented development is the current silver bullet being touted by the trade journals as the solution to the IS programming backlog. Rumors prevail that this is a revolutionary way of looking at the systems development process. However, object-oriented concepts may prove to be an *evolutionary* rather than *revolutionary* shift. With object-oriented development, both data and programming logic act upon the data, and are grouped together in what is called an object. Discussion of what object-oriented development is, and how it is accomplished, is beyond the scope of this book. Many of the client/server applications being developed today are based on object-oriented techniques.

This technology's main benefit is the reduction of application development time. However, before a process is automated the same underlying issue remains to be answered—is the system or process necessary? By concentrating on reducing the programming backlog without regard to this question, the organization as a whole will not benefit. The information systems department may reduce its programming backlog, but if ineffective or obsolete processes are automated, the organization has lost the opportunity to redesign itself. Though systems can be developed more quickly, or are changed more easily, there is no major benefit if the underlying business process was ineffective in the first place and should have been radically altered or eliminated? Using object-oriented technology it is quicker and easier to develop a custom-programmed application. If outsourcing is a viable outcome from a business process redesign effort, has the company profited from applying this technology?

Before seeking technologies continually address the issue of whether a process should exist, or should be radically altered. There is a temptation to implement automated systems quickly, without fully understanding the business processes the automated system should model. However, a potential problem that may result from the ability to quickly and easily develop computer applications is that more and more automated systems may be introduced into the organization that are built upon outdated business processes. With more capital invested in automated systems that model the current business processes, it is more difficult to cost-justify, in the short term, radically altering existing business processes. Object-oriented analysis, design, and programming is a viable alternative to traditional automated system development, given existing business processes have been redesigned first. A suggested reading list is available at the end of this chapter if you are interested in further exploring this or any of the other technologies discussed in this appendix.

Wireless and Mobile Computing

Wireless computing allows information to be readily accessible to anyone in the organization, wherever they are. Telephone pager systems can be consolidated with voice mail and e-mail systems to alert individuals to an incoming message. Notebook or palm top computers can be connected to cellular phones to transmit data just about anywhere in the world from just about anywhere. This technology can implement radically altered business processes. The physical limitations of an office need not be a consideration in a redesigned business process. Point-of-sale systems can now be mobile. The need for data entry systems and buildings where data entry clerks enter sales information can be replaced with a mobile sales force entering information directly into the corporate database. This technology enables business processes to be redesigned without the constraints of buildings or the pre-existing communications infrastructure (phone lines).

Information Highway (Internet)

The information highway promises international data communications. The Internet is the main lane of this superhighway. The Internet is not one large network; it is comprised of many networks linked together and maintained independently. This technology enables organizations to consider connecting geographically distributed offices. The information highway is a concept endorsed by the current U.S. Administration and will provide a communications (data, voice, and graphics) infrastructure enabling more cooperation between businesses and between business and education. Most universities are currently connected to the Internet with more corporate or commercial organizations connecting every day.

Geographic location is no longer a constraint when redesigning processes. In the past, organizations located accounting departments in one place, marketing or manufacturing staff in other locations. Those individuals that needed to continually communicate with one another and share information were physically located together. However, with the ability to connect offices anywhere around the globe, marketing need not be physically centralized, nor does accounting or personnel. Both the Internet and wireless communications provide for redesigning processes without the physical limitations of location.

Converging Technologies (voice, image, data)

Various technologies such as voice, video , and data are converging. Technologies supporting solutions incorporating voice and data are possible today. Many applications and vendor products support integrating telephone and paging services with computer databases and e-mail services. The line separating telephone and voice technology with computer and data technology is beginning to blur. Redesigned business processes which would not have been technically feasible 10 years ago can be accomplished today. Most redesign efforts are not limited by the technology, but by inertia and resistance to change within organizations. Once you have determined what the redesigned system should accomplish, how to accomplish it requires sorting through the various technologies to find one that meets your needs.

EFFECTS ENABLING TECHNOLOGIES HAVE ON BPR

Technology currently exists that can implement almost any type of change or redesigned business process. Processes which could not be changed in the past because available technology was limited, can now freely be explored and radically changed. Twenty years ago, business processes could not have been redesigned to allow a mobile sales force to enter data at the time of sale into a corporate database; now this is not only possible but is also being accomplished by many organizations. Telecommunications and database technology have advanced to a point to make this a reality. Current downsized, distributed computing environments, as well as advances in telecommunications, allow various process redesign possibilities to be explored. Using the Internet or wireless communications along with notebook computers and portable phones, an organization could virtually exist without a central office.

Once again, the temptation to redesign processes to take advantage of latest technologies must be resisted. There must be sound underlying business reasons for changing existing business processes. The outcome or goal of any redesign project should not be to utilize the latest technology, but to solve a business problem or to take advantage of a competitive edge in the market. If this can be done by exploiting the newest technology, so much the better. However, new technology should not be the driving force in business process redesign projects.

To summarize, technologies should be viewed as enabling change, not driving it. Many technologies have been invented for one purpose and used for another. For instance, Edison's phonograph was thought to be an automation solution for the office dictation process; however, its ultimate use was for playing music. New technologies are continuously being invented and imaginative applications pursued. The current presumption of what these technologies could/should be used for may not be correct. Continual scanning of new technologies coupled with breakthrough thinking will allow business processes and business systems to be changed or redesigned in ways that were not technically feasible before.

Suggested readings for further information on the topics covered in this chapter are:

Ed Krol, *The Whole Internet*.

Tracy LaQuey, *Internet Companions Guide*.

Michael Banks, *Portable Communications*.

W. H. Inmon, *Developing Client/Server Applications*.

Gilbert Held, *Understanding Data Communications*.

Mark von Wodtke, *Mind Over Media*.

Peter Coad and Edward Yourdan, *Object-Oriented Analysis*.

David W. Embley, Barry D. Kurtz, and Scott N. Woodfield, *Object-Oriented Systems Analysis*.

(Full bibliographic information is given in the References at the end of this book.)

References

Banks, Michael A. *Portable Communications: The Traveling Executives Survival Guide.* New York: Brady Publishing, 1992.

Barcomb, David. *Office Automation: A Survey of Tools and Technology, 2d ed.* Bedford, Mass.: Digital Press, 1989.

Barker, Joel Arthur. *Discovering the Future: The Business of Paradigms.* St. Paul, Minn.: ILI Press, 1988.

Boone, Mary E. *Leadership and the Computer.* Rocklin, Cal.: Prima Publishing, 1991.

Carr, Clay. *Smart Training: The Manager's Guide to Training for Improved Performance.* New York: McGraw Hill, 1992.

Chase, Richard B., and Nicholas J. Aquilano. *Production and Operations Management: A Life Cycle Approach.* Homewood, Ill.: Irwin, 1989.

Cleland, David I., and Karen M. Bursic. *Strategic Technology Management: Systems for Products and Processes.* New York: AMACOM, 1992.

Coad, Peter, and Edward Yourdon. *Object-Oriented Analysis, 2d ed.* Englewood Cliffs, N.J.: Yourdon Press, 1991.

DeMarco, Tom, and Tim Lister. *Controlling Software Projects.* Englewood Cliffs, N.J.: Prentice-Hall, 1976.

Dinsmore, Paul C. *Human Factors in Project Management, rev. ed.* New York: AMACOM, 1990.

Drucker, Peter F. *Management Tasks, Responsibilities, Practices.* New York: Harper & Row, 1979.

Embley, David W., Barry D. Kurtz, and Scott N. Woodfield. *Object-Oriented Systems Analysis: A Model-Driven Approach.* Englewood Cliffs, N.J.: Yourdon Press, 1992.

Friend, David. "Understanding Cooperative Processing." *Information Technologies.* (May 1993):22–28.

Gane, Chris, and Trish Sarson. *Structured Systems Analysis: Tools and Techniques.* Englewood Cliffs, N.J.: Prentice-Hall, 1979.

Gibson, Cyrus, and Barbara Bund Jackson. *The Information Imperative.* Lexington, Mass.: D. C. Heath and Company, Lexington Books, 1987.

Hammer, Michael. *Harvard Business Review.* 1990.

Held, Gilbert. *Understanding Data Communications, 3d ed.* Carmel, Ind.: SAMS, 1991.

Hershey, Gerald L., and Donna Kizzier. *Planning and Implementing End-User Information Systems: Office and End-User Systems Management.* Cincinnati: South-Western Publishing, 1992.

Hickman, Craig, and Michael Silva. *Creating Excellence: Management Corporate Culture, Strategy and Change in the New Age.* New York: Plume, 1984.

Inmon, W. H. *Developing Client / Server Applications.* Wellesley, Mass.: QED, 1993.

Kanter, Rosabeth Moss. *When Giants Learn to Dance.* New York: Simon and Schuster, 1989.

Koulopoulos, Thomas M. "The Document Factory: Part I." *Inform.* (June 1993):42–46.

Koulopoulos, Thomas M. "The Document Factory: Part II." *Inform.* (July 1993):44–47.

Krol, Ed. *The Whole Internet: User's Guide & Catalog.* Sebastopol, Cal.: O'Reilly & Assoc., 1992.

Kubeck, Lynn C. *The Decentralization of Programming Development.* End User Computing Management. New York: Auerbach, 1993.

LaQuey, Tracy. *The Internet Companion: A Beginner's Guide to Global Networking.* Reading, Mass.: Addison-Wesley, 1993.

Larson, Richard W., and David J. Zimney. *The White Collar Shuffle: Who Does What in Today's Computerized Workplace.* New York: AMACOM, 1990.

Martin, James. *Information Engineering: Book I, Introduction.* Englewood Cliffs, N.J.: Prentice-Hall, 1989.

Martin, James. *Information Engineering: Book II, Planning and Analysis.* Englewood Cliffs, N.J.: Prentice-Hall, 1989.

Martin, James. *Information Engineering: Book III, Design & Construction.* Englewood Cliffs, N.J.: Prentice-Hall, 1989.

Martin, James, and Joel Leben. *Strategic Information Planning Methodologies, 2d ed.* Englewood Cliffs, N.J.: Prentice-Hall, 1989.

Martin, James, and James J. Odell. *Object-Oriented Analysis and Design.* Englewood Cliffs, N.J.: Prentice-Hall, 1992.

Martin, James, and James J. Odell. *Principles of Object-Oriented Analysis and Design.* Englewood Cliffs, N.J.: Prentice-Hall, 1993.

Mitroff, Ian I., and Harold A. Linstone. *The Unbounded Mind: Breaking the Chains of Traditional Business Thinking.* New York: Oxford University Press, 1993.

Neusch, Donna R., and Alan F. Siebenaler. *The High Performance Enterprise: Reinventing the People Side of Your Business.* Essex Junction, Vt.: Oliver Wight Publications, 1993.

Parsaye, Kamran, Mark Chignell, Setrag Khoshafian, and Harry Wong. *Intelligent Databases: Object-Oriented, Deductive Hypermedia Technologies.* New York: John Wiley, 1989.

Peters, Tom. *Thriving on Chaos.* New York: Harper & Row, 1987.

Rentzel, Thomas. "Synergy In the Next Century — Part II The Process." *Inform.* (June 1993):55–64.

Rothschild, Michael. *The Coming Productivity Surge.* Forbes ASAP, 1993.

Rubin, Howard. "Is Your Software Engineering Lost in Space?" *Chief Information Officer.* (July/August 1993):29–32.

Smith, Harold T., William H. Baker, Mary Sumner, and Almon J. Bate. *Automated Office Systems Management.* New York: John Wiley, 1985.

Steenis, Hein van. *How to Plan, Develop & Use Information Systems: A Guide to Human Qualities and Productivity.* New York: Dorset House Publishing, 1990.

Tomasko, Robert. *Downsizing: Reshaping the Corporation for the Future.* New York: AMACOM, 1990.

von Wodtke, Mark. *Mind Over Media: Creative Thinking Skills for Electronic Media.* New York: McGraw Hill, 1993.

Weinberg, Gerald M. *Rethinking Systems Analysis & Design.* New York: Dorset House Publishing, 1988.

Westin, Alan F., Heather A. Schweder, Michael A. Baker, and Sheila Lehman. *The Changing Workplace: A Guide to Managing the People, Organizational and Regulatory Aspects of Office Technology.* New York: Knowledge Industry Publications, 1985.

Whitten, Jeffrey L., Lonnie D. Bentley, and Victor M. Barlow. *Systems Analysis & Design Methods, 3d ed.* Burr Ridge, Ill.: Irwin, 1994.

Yourdon, E. *Decline & Fall of the American Programmer.* Englewood Cliffs, N.J.: Yourdon Press, 1992.

Yourdon, E. *Managing the Systems Development Life Cycle.* New York: Yourdon Press, 1980.

Zuboff, Shoshana. *In the Age of the Smart Machine.* New York: Basic Books, 1988.

Index